look at me

Also by Nataniël

Dancing with John (1992)
Oopmond (1993)
Nataniël kook (1994)
Rubber (1996)
Die Nataniël-kombuis (1996)
Maria Maria (1999)
Tuesday (2001)
Food from the White House (2002)
Kaalkop (2004)
Kaalkop Journal/Joernaal (2006)
Kaalkop² (2008)
When I Was (2008)
Gatherings (2009)
Nicky & Lou (2011)
Kaalkop 3 (2012)
150 stories (2014)
Die huis van rye (2015)
Zip! (2016)
Closet (2017)
Die Edik van Nantes-kookboek (2018)

look at me

NATANIËL

recollections of a childhood

Translated from the original Afrikaans by Iolandi Pool

Human & Rousseau

First published in 2019 by Human & Rousseau,
an imprint of NB Publishers,
a division of Media24 Boeke (Pty) Ltd
40 Heerengracht, Cape Town, South Africa

Front-cover photograph by Eben le Roux
Back-cover photograph by Clinton Lubbe
Cover design by Albino Creations
Page design by Michiel Botha
Set in 11 pt on 15 pt Minion

Originally printed in South Africa
ISBN: 978-0-7981-7996-6 (First edition, first impression 2019)

LSiPOD: 978-0-7981-8001-6 (Second edition, first impression 2019)
ISBN: 978-0-7981-7997-3 (epub)
ISBN: 978-0-7981-7998-0 (mobi)

For Madri
who was only born somewhere between pages 260 and 261

Sand

What should your earliest memory be? What do you remember as your very first scene? Is it you in the chicken run in Wellington? You are sitting on the ground among the chickens, your mouth is wide open, Grandfather is holding something out to you, a pebble or an earthworm, and you are planning on eating it – you eat everything. No, that's the photo in Mother's album, the family still laughs about it. Is it you swinging on the garden gate, a floppy hat on your head? That was during a visit to the Langkloof, at your cousin Magdel's home. No, that's another black-and-white photo from the album. Is it you and your blow-up dog, with all the boys from the children's home in Riebeek East? No, another photo, examined a thousand times.

Is it perhaps the sound of rain on the roof? The roof was corrugated iron and rain was scarce and like music. Is it the rustle of leaves in the big tree in front of the house? You've just woken up on your patchwork quilt and are looking at the gigantic dark branches, crossing one another with sharp elbows, a maze in the sky, a mysterious space inhabited by tiny characters known only to you. It would be lovely if your story could begin like this.

Sand. That is what I remember. The smell of sand. Old sand. This sand has been trucked in from far away, a long, long time ago. It fills a sandpit, round and twice as big as a fishpond. The pit has a cement rim with bits of slate set into it, awkwardly and sloppily, a circle of dark-grey stains. This is my play area. I sit on the sand. In front of me are two fat little legs with dimpled knees. They lie straight, like a doll's. I follow them to my torso. These are *my* legs. (He sits like the dead! Grandmother always said.) Yes, sitting was my thing. Long after my cousins of the same age were walking and talking, I still sat. (But when he *started* it was all over! Grandmother always said.)

Around me are plastic buckets and shovels in every colour. Now and then I stick a shovel in the sand and unearth another lump. Petrified cat poo. That's where the unique smell comes from. Old sand with old poo makes for a smell that I will still recognise in designer gardens forty years later. I don't think Mother would have let me play there if she knew the pit was an irresistible ablution facility for the neighbourhood's night cats, but how could she have known? Cats bury and I sit with little shovels.

There in front of the house is my father. He's trimming the edges of the lawn. He is tall and strong and very handsome. His arms bulge like in a drawing when he works in the garden. Schoolgirls and their mothers smile and say hello when they walk by, then they giggle and whisper to each other. I can see this from the pit.

On the porch is my mother. She is very pretty, she has dark women's hair (women's hair: not straight, not curly, not short, not long, just to the neck with the merest presence of a soft wave) and a tiny waist. She is dressed in a gleaming white blouse with short sleeves and a wide skirt with big flowers. She puts a small bowl on the porch wall.

Here's a bit of biltong, she says. Eat slowly.

She walks back into the house to check if my little brother is still sleeping. It was a small, small house, to me it was a big, big house. There were five steps from the sandpit to the porch, a cool porch with a polished cement floor and the same pitched roof as the rest of the house, always cool. Inside was a passageway, to the left was Father and Mother's room, my little brother's bed was also there, further down the passage was the door to my room, a big room with, behind a second door, its own toilet and washbasin. At the end of the passage was the bathroom. To the right of the front door was the lounge, then a door to the dining room, here lay the newspaper. Then the kitchen with a table in the middle and a window above the sink.

The sun moves behind the tree and a ray of light hits my face. Squinting, I look up. I am showered in golden dust.

Did you read the label? a voice yells, shrill and hysterical. You can't just throw it!

I forgot! says a second voice, this one is thin and quavering.

Read it now! What does it say?

Appetite!

The child already has an enormous appetite! He was born like that! Do you realise what the rest of his life is going to look like?

I'm sorry!

I blink my eyes. I can't see anyone. Again I am showered in golden dust.

Now I've given him Fear, says the shrill voice, I could see on his suitcase he was born without it. You have one more bottle, first read the label!

It's Doubt, says the quavering voice.

Yes, that's right. It's sad, but go ahead, throw!

Again the golden dust. Through the glitter I see something flutter. Something moves out of the sun and circles above my head. A dragonfly? No, I see a tiny face. A lean body hangs from two see-through wings, I see dark hair and a delicate dress that flickers, coppery and sparkling. I have never seen anything like this, but I know it's a fairy. There is a second flapping creature, a heavy little body that struggles to stay in the air, up and down, fall and rise, the dainty wings flap fiercely, the light hair tangles in the little face. Her dress is pinkish-white and bunches around her like a cocoon.

I have one more bottle, says the first fairy with the shrill voice. It's Rage. Without this he'll be defenceless.

Golden dust gleams in the ray of light.

Becca! she yells. Where are you?

Here! says the second voice.

I turn my head. The heavy one is flapping round and round the bowl of biltong on the porch wall.

I am so hungry, she says, I'll just take one bite.

It's meat! yells the brunette.

Meat?

The child's mother put it there! They eat dried meat! Do you realise what's going to happen now?

Bora! screams the heavy fairy.

She falls from the sky, behind the porch wall, I can't see what is happening.

There's a flash of copper, the light fairy dives down to the bowl of biltong and hangs upside down. Is she also eating? Suddenly she shoots into the air.

Becca! she yells.

She too drops behind the porch wall.

Mommmm! I yell.

I hear strange noises, someone gasps for air, something rips, someone sobs, someone sighs. Two human figures appear from behind the porch wall, one tall, one short, one thin, one round, one with stringy dark hair, one with a messy bush of blonde hair.

Daaaddddd!

The figures stumble down the steps, each with her arms wrapped around herself, trying to keep the ripped dresses together. Like people who have never walked, they lift their feet high and struggle with big steps to the garden gate.

My mother comes running out the front door, my father appears from the back of the house.

What's going on? asks my mother. Why is your head shining?

I point. The garden gate is open. Two figures waddle up the hill.

You don't have to be scared, says my mother. They're probably just collecting. They could have closed the gate at least – manners, manners.

One day my mother puts my baby brother in his pram, buckles me into my dark-red sandals and takes my hand. The three of us go up the hill to the big house on the other side of the vineyard. The big house doesn't have a garden gate like normal houses, just a gate for cars, no car. We walk through the small crowd of lemon trees covered with golden-yellow ovals, each tree a giant lantern. The porch curves round three sides of the house, it's a wide porch full of couches covered in blankets, shelves of jars without lids, rows and rows of pot plants (each pot is different and most are cracked or have sacrificed a big chip), garden boots and bunches of dried herbs. The side of the house faces the street, the front looks out over the vineyard to our home. On this side of the porch stands a wooden table with a jug of ice-cold lemonade and a patterned plate of ginger biscuits. (On later visits, I realised that lemonade was always waiting, always ice-cold, even when guests weren't expected. The biscuits – which looked exactly like ginger biscuits should look, not too flat or too pale or with too few cracks, exactly right – were always fresh from the oven. How was that possible?)

On that first day, the front door is open. This door consists of a series of wooden frames filled with crinkly glass and is never closed again, for as long as we live in our house; through wind and weather, heat and hail, day or night it is open. Tall and slender with a dark braid and a straight, ankle-length dress of copper velvet, that's what she looks like, the oldish woman who is waiting for us. She greets us warmly, kisses my baby brother on his forehead and takes my face in her hands.

What a lovely boy! she says. And look at those golden curls!

Yes, we have no idea where this hair suddenly came from, says my mother, Definitely not from the family.

Come in, the woman says, My sister is in the kitchen, you can't get her out of there.

We walk down a passage full of strange objects, globes on silver stands, birdcages with open doors, lamps without light bulbs and upright containers full of pitch-black umbrellas with wooden handles carved into faces. The kitchen is big and full of food, almost as much food as in Grandmother's kitchen. There are high, cheerful windows with crocheted curtains, the walls in between are overgrown with narrow shelves buckling under rows and rows of glass jars, every fruit and vegetable you can think of has been preserved. Tins without lids display mountains of rusks, a tray is loaded with fruit loaf and pots steam on a big stove.

The sister is round as a ball and also oldish. Her light-pink dress is wrinkled, she's lost a button, one sleeve is unravelling and most of her snow-white hair has already escaped a crooked bun. She is holding on to a chair and does not look at my mother or my little brother: she is talking just to me.

You must be hungry, she says in a shaky voice, Sit down, what do you like? We have pies and pancakes and I've bottled some peaches.

We have everything, laughs the tall woman, She never stops.

I stayed and ate until my mother said we *have* to go now. After that I was there every second day, or as often as my mother allowed. The Stoepsusters (one was always on the porch, the other never) asked questions, listened, cried, sang, warned, fed and called each other Sister. I talked, ate, laughed a lot and wondered even more.

Many years later, I was grocery shopping one day with Grandmother in Wellington. We were on our way to the car, two women came out of the butchery, one was tall, the other short, both dressed in long dresses from another era. Unsteady on their feet, they held on to each other. One woman's shoes were worn through, the other's hair was a mess, one held a packet wrapped in brown paper; on her finger was an unusual ring with a big stone, on the other's shoulder was a sprinkling of fine sequins like she was at a concert or a wild party.

I looked at Grandmother.

Yes, she sighed. That's what happens when fairies eat meat.

Our Fence

Our World and the Whole World were separated only by silver chicken wire. The holes were big and the wire was thin, the kind that wouldn't keep anything in or out, it was just there, stretched tightly between thin silver poles, a shoulder-high, almost invisible fence, where else should silver wire go? The fence ran along three sides of the erf, at the front by the road, on one side along the empty erf between the Gagianos and us, and on the other side alongside the vineyard that belonged to nobody. There was no fence at the back of the erf. There was a back yard with a shed full of tools, and a cement laundry block, complete with a high tap and a deep basin. Trees, some fruit-bearing and others not, stood around like creatures that were unwilling to either chat or queue. Long grass and single reed stalks showed that the erf had come to an end, here there was a small vlei, sometimes a trickle of water burbled quietly.

I never questioned the purpose of the fence, it wasn't for safety, what danger could there be? And at the back it was unnecessary, beyond the vlei there was nothing, the Whole World ended there, as it did two streets away on the other side of town, as it did at the end of our friends' erf downtown. (Our Whole World was called a town, there were other towns too, those existed only when we went there. The rest of the time they were their own Whole Worlds.)

On hot days I stood on the front porch and watched the fence glitter in the sun, it was a spider's web without a fly, with a small front gate, also glittering, and a big gate for cars. The brilliant shine was because the fence had been painted, why and by whom a fence made of chicken wire had been painted was a mystery, it was covered in the shiniest paint anyone had ever seen. And it was neat. And because it was neat, nothing grew on it, not a single climber stretched out a tendril, the spider's web hung there, empty and clean.

And here a child could do what has long since become impossible: even early in your life you could open the small gate and step into the Whole World. You could walk on your own down the road, right in the middle, traffic was scarce and it was quiet. Grandmother said you could hear a motor car the moment it left the factory, you would know when you had to make way.

The Whole World was called Riebeek-Kasteel. And when you stood at the gate and looked to your left, up the hill, you saw The Stoepsusters' house, the stop street and the crossroad. On the other side were orchards full of shadows and a sheltered house where someone with a title lived, Reverend, Sergeant, Magistrate, the kind of man whose wife was never seen without a brooch. I liked looking to the right. There the downward slope levelled out, you could walk to the corner erf. Here I often played. I have no idea who lived there, but I knew the garden well, an exceptionally big, empty yard without a single blade of grass, only rose bushes, millions of them, in between were fountains and benches. The house was in the middle of all the roses, a long, flat house with Venetian blinds, repulsive and always shut, I can't remember ever going inside.

When you turned right, a tennis court and an empty square were on your left, this was the centre of town. Here farmers parked their bakkies. I knew what farmers were and that they lived on farms and that their children also lived there and disappeared from the town every afternoon after school, but as long as the town was the Whole World, I didn't feel like thinking about it or trying to understand where the farms fitted in.

As soon as the police station appeared on your right, you could turn left to the shops. This was a concoction of buildings, porches, alleys, courtyards and a few houses, all connected. First was the haberdashery, it belonged to a friendly woman, she was as thin as a rail and every day her long, pitch-black leg hair was flattened by stockings, people called it blanket legs. There was a post office and next to it an alleyway with doors to rooms where single people lived, also a back yard full of the middle shop owner's children. I played here occasionally, but when I had 20c in my hand I walked straight into the shop. The middle shop's inside was made of wood. Counters with glass fronts wound through the entire space and displayed the contents of their drawers. Screws, sweets, gloves, blue soap, polish, cooldrink glasses, socks, ties, toys, apricot sweets, marshmallow fish, pocketknives, nappies, fly poison, clothes pegs, tomato sauce, envelopes, writing pads, pencils, curtain hooks, hinges, sunglasses and headache powders, all in a row.

In this shop I discovered that a day without possibility, even the smallest explosion of deliciousness, was an unbearable greyness. As soon as I knew the way, I begged my mother to send me there, and she did, two or three times a week, to buy something, always two things at a time: a loaf of bread and a bottle of milk. Or a bag of tomatoes and a newspaper. Or orange squash and brown paper. Then there was 5c left over. With this I could buy myself two things: a vienna and a small bag of chips. I was a rich man's child! Add Saturday's hot dogs and Sunday's pudding, and there was seldom a day without a highlight.

If you didn't turn left at the rose garden but went straight ahead, you would walk past the small haunted house, a miniature house with boarded-up windows and a closed-off porch right on the road. There was nobody here. And nobody talked about it. Then you could turn right again, just after the tennis court and the parking place for the farmers with farms that for now were located in another world; then you were in the high street, even though the street you had just been in was called High Street.

But we carry straight on. On the next corner was a garage. Here my father worked, he was one of the town's mechanics and could fix anything, if anything moved in town it was because of my father, everyone said he was the best in the district. What was a district? Where did a district fit in the Whole World? I never asked, it was enough that Father was the best.

Here the untarred road began, and also the hill, church, school, dormitory, all in a row. Then downhill again, then a side street to the right. Here everyone turned without looking to the left for even a moment; just before you turned, just after the empty piece

of ground next to the dormitory, lived The Vuurhoutjies. Whoever thought up the word *boskasie* must have gone past there first.
Trees like you wouldn't see anywhere else grew there, twisted and
bent in all directions, like crazy ballerinas they formed a circle
around a hut of clay, stone, cement, wood and corrugated iron,
not a squatter's shack, a crooked magician's cocoon with an appeal
no one could withstand, once you looked you stopped, you were
transfixed. The dirtiest family in the Whole World lived there, they
were called The Vuurhoutjies because their faces were all black as
soot. They did have water, also electricity, also clothes, they just
didn't feel like it. Food simmered in a pot over a fire, a goat bleated,
a sheep wailed, chickens scratched, a pack of children wandered
about, wrapped in blankets or tied up in towels, all with long, shaggy
hair, not young children, teenagers, lovely, muscled, dirty teenagers
who went to school when they felt like it, sometimes came to stand
in the door during a church service, slunk around late at night,
never did any harm, only prowled and growled like wolves.

Turn right, quickly turn right. Twenty steps from The Vuurhoutjies
there was a big erf we often visited, here Uncle Sam and Aunt
Stienie lived. Aunt Stienie was Grandmother's sister, a tiny, sweet
woman whose face I could never remember, every time my
mother had to introduce her to me again. Uncle Sam was big and
busy in the yard, everywhere there were piles of raw material,
countless projects patiently awaited their completion. There was
also gardening, rows of vegetables flourished in the sun, and
chickens were slaughtered, yes, the first time I unsuspectingly
stood closer when a hen was laid down on a tree stump. Here
comes a trick, I thought. Long after the head was gone and the
feet stopped jerking, I stood by the pile of tarred poles, throwing
up and sobbing in turn.

What I do remember with pleasure is the darkness of the house, a big house with a long passage. It was a good darkness, Aunt Stienie's victory over the heat, she could darken a room so completely with long curtains – were there shutters or blinds as well? – that I couldn't believe the coolness. I remember one time when the house was completely silent, there was a corpse in the corner room, the hearse had to come from far away, from a place that only existed when a hearse was needed, and this was the coolest house imaginable. Was it a family member? Or just an acquaintance with nowhere else to wait? I do not know, but I do remember the peaceful occasion, calm and full of acceptance; to me it was entirely new and I liked it. It was like factory custard nowadays, deadly *and* delicious and nobody talks about it.

A year after my memory found me, I still don't know how many questions each person is allowed, these conclusions are thus my own:

It doesn't take long to explore our town,
only occasionally surprising,
pretty enough,
bedtime feels a little too early,
at the moment everyone has enough to eat.
Thank you.

So it was in the two worlds on either side of the neatest unfinished fence in history.

Boys

No idea where they came from, but they were often there. To play under the big tree next to the garage. There the soil wasn't like in the sandpit, we could build houses and dig trenches.

Like most first-borns, my bedroom was filled with toys, everything parents could think of was there in crates and cupboards. I myself could think of many other things, much better objects with which to entertain and educate myself, but for the moment I had to be satisfied with those things suitable for little boys. And as far as toys for boys went, I was only interested in the packaging.

Cars were my father's entire being and at some stage miniature automobiles, colourful, with a shiny finish and completely true to life, began appearing on shops' shelves. Fathers and sons lost their minds and spinning tops, catapults, rubber animals and wooden trucks were cast aside. My father had to lose his mind without me, but he still carted a fleet into my bedroom.

I wasn't ungrateful – every small thing with wheels was packaged in a colourful cardboard box with a see-through plastic window. These new boxes smelled of the factory, they were brand new with sharp corners and printed scenes and designs. I was very impressed with these offerings from a tiny world of glamour, I set them out in formations and held exhibitions lit with my bedside lamp and my flashlight. All of these automobiles, sports cars, bakkies, buses, bulldozers or lorries were called cars.

Go get your cars! Your friends are here!

What friends?

Each time I wanted to explain to my parents that my friends were already around me, couldn't they see anything, but then the house angel would appear from somewhere and whisper in my ear: They aren't ready yet.

Perhaps my mother wanted to start an after-school centre, perhaps my father paid their parents, but the boys were there, under the tree, two, three times a week. We had our cars, shovels, buckets of water, scraps of wood from the storeroom and bottles of cooldrink with blue paper straws. We graded roads, mixed mud, built houses, riverbanks and shops. I built the church. Every time. With a bell and a small verger in front of the door.

Next to me a boy pushes a red thing with a red trailer past the row of houses.

Gggrrrooooommmm, he goes.

Are you a lion? I ask.

My pistons are broken, he says.

I am going to tell my mother you swore.

This lorry really pulls, he says.

You are going to break the path, I say. Don't drive so close to the houses, play neatly!

Wwhhrrr! growls another child.

Shh! I say. They are praying in church!

I need rope, says the child with the golden head. He has short, rock-hard golden-yellow hair, each strand leaning forward like a little soldier bowing before a king.

We don't have rope, I say.

If I tie my straw to this lorry, it's a cannon, he says.

A cannon is for war, I say.

War is coming, says the golden head, They want to take our things.

Who?

The people in the location, he says.

We have to build a wall, says the one with the red trailer, High, high, high!

We can smash everything before they come! another one yells, very excited.

What is a location? I ask.

Every town has a location, says the golden head, They want our things, my dad says.

You aren't playing right, I say, You can't make cannons! And you can't smash things!

We can play how we like!

You can't! I say, And you have to polish your cars! Yours are always dirty and dusty!

You're stupid, says the golden head.

You're stupid!

I'm going now, I'm not playing here again!

Me neither!

Me neither!

They are gone, I am relieved, I run to the kitchen: in the bottom drawer are two tiny light-blue bows, my mother took them off my brother's baby jersey. I run back. I grab a white car and put it in front of the church. Carefully I put the bows on the bonnet. Wedding car.

Day One

: Can he hear us?

: No, he's in his room. Where's your little one?

: At the neighbours', they have an inflatable pool, I can't keep him away from there.

: What are we going to do? It's only a couple of weeks still!

: What can you do? You can't run away, you can't make time stop, we've gone ahead and bought the clothes.

: So have we, not everything yet, we have to go again. It's not going to lessen the shock, but at least you can keep an eye on him when he tries things on, or sees the tiny school case, maybe there's something that tells you if he's going to be one of The Lucky Ones.

: I know! But we couldn't figure out much. He was crazy about the tie that clips on, he even put it on again in the car. And the shoes!

He keeps saying he's big now. Like his cousins.

: We've considered just blatantly lying about his age and keeping him back a year, at least it gives you time.

: Yes, luckily they're not some of those tall children.

: They are so little!

: Maybe the laws will change. You always hear about things happening. Some of them stay home now.

: Those are the rich people, they can do anything.

: What about The Prince? When The Prince comes, everything is different!

: When has The Prince ever come here? We only hear about others who are saved in faraway places, never a place we know.

: They say he makes some disappear, others go to places that have been set up just for them, some live *and* learn under domes, *with* their families, imagine that! Only The Merciful can see them!

: We can only hope! And ask around! It's safe to ask, right?

: We'll manage something. I won't let my child perish.

: My child is special, none of this lot is going to know what he needs.

: Where are you, Prince?

This conversation never took place. They were in the lounge, my mother, my father, Derick's mother and father. I was in the passage and could hear everything, they talked about the price of school clothes, who would drop off and pick up the children until they were old enough to walk by themselves, it really wasn't far. And it would be completely safe if they walked together. And keep out of the road if a car came. Except if it rained, of course. And then there were things like sport and choir practice, but that would surely only start in a year or two. So they talked, but The Conversation never took place. How could it? They didn't know about it. Neither did I. I only wrote it down recently, The Conversation All Parents Should Have Before Children Are Sent To School, Especially If Children With Fairy Dust Are The Topic Of Discussion.

And The Prince? No one knew about him then.

And so, a few weeks later, without intervention, without trumpets and heralds announcing the new rules, absolutely ordinary, as if it were completely natural, the school year begins. Day One starts like we're on a ship, my mother looks like she always does, my father too, the house hasn't lost its shape, but everything else is strange, I am unsteady on my feet, the world wobbles. I am wearing my new clothes, white shirt, thin grey jersey, grey shorts, grey socks, black shoes. (Now I realise they might have been other colours, but all the photos from those years were black and white, thus I am all in grey.)

In my hand is a school case, a hard, small brown suitcase. Inside is a lunchbox with sandwiches, also a square plastic bottle with red cooldrink, a handkerchief, an apple, two big books, one with light-blue lines, one without, and a small bag with coloured pencils. I like my school case a lot, it smells brand new. I open the lid and turn back to my closet.

No, no, says my mother, You don't have to take any toys, they have everything. Come along, we don't want to be late.

It is a terrible thing when something familiar suddenly comes to life and shows you that you knew nothing, you are caught unawares. We have gone past the school a hundred times, it is between the church and the dormitory, on the way to three regular places we went visiting, but today it swallows us up, in at the tiny gate, up the stairs, past a hall, round a corner, past a pillar, another pillar, children, children, children, into a classroom. Here is your chair, here is your desk, here are your parents, they are now strangers, they are going to leave you right here, look at them laugh, talk to other strangers, they wave to you, you don't wave back, you look down. What is rubbing like that? It is the block around your neck, a dark-grey, flattish, rough block, it presses against your stomach, scratches your throat, it's your fear, from now on it will always be with you, no, you're not sleepy, no, you're not weak, no, your legs are strong enough, it is only the block that's still new, yes, the nausea is completely natural, you will get used to it, you are drifting now, like you're on a ship, the ship is swaying on the sea, on the ship is a swimming pool, it is also swaying and you are in that water. You are swaying along with the sway of the sway. You are not dying, you are just not touching the ground. You hear everything your teacher says and you do what you must, she is one of The Merciful, she sees you, she sees you are drifting, but she cannot stop it, she must do her job.

I liked Miss Van Wyk a lot, she was friendly, not friendly enough to say school is over now, but she did have compassion. (Those were Grandmother's words, if someone showed you compassion, you were safe.) In a photo in my album I am sitting next to her, you can't see at all that I'm drifting, I am smiling broadly. On my chest is a paper face with my name.

What I like a lot, despite the ship and its swaying and the block around my neck and my parents who are missing, is the smell in the classroom. Powder paint, starch paint, watercolours, plasticine, crayons, glue, wooden blocks, wooden beads, paper of every thickness and texture, together all of this creates a smell that I will recognise for the rest of my life in studios and workshops, the places where craftsmen slave away to give shape to something unrecognisable or unreachable.

From somewhere comes a voice I don't know, a man's voice, he is talking to me, softly and calmly: It's not so bad, see? It's not that bad at all.

Outside someone rings a bell. Miss Van Wyk makes us stand in a row.

Are we going home now? I ask. But the block presses against my throat and makes my voice hoarse, nobody hears me.

It's break time, says Miss. We are all going to walk together to the trees, there you can play and eat your sandwiches. If someone wants to go to the bathroom, just tell me and I will walk with you.

So I learn a term that holds more fear and cruelty than any ghost story Grandfather could ever think up. Break time. My block is heavy, I struggle to breathe, I just follow the child in front of me. I don't look up, I only see shoes, there must be more than a million, all the shoes look like mine, I look up slightly, everyone's clothes also look like mine, why? So we can disappear like those pieces of my puzzle with the big sky? My mother and father will never come to look for me, they are at home with my baby brother. Why do they want me gone? And these children! Why are they yelling so? And jumping like goats? Don't they know we've been thrown to the wolves? (Also Grandmother's words.)

Here I learn another thing, suspense. I drift, now among the million identical children, nobody hurts me, nobody says any-thing funny, nobody grabs my sandwich, but I'm waiting for it, there is no one who can help me here, Miss can't watch everybody, why is there a break? Why must you leave your desk and your case? Surely you can play at home!

I look up. No, look down! There are bigger children at the building with the toilets. They are watching us. I chew my sandwich. I like eating, but here I taste nothing.

The day lasts another thousand hours. I don't know how I got home. I have a star on my forehead and a drawing in my hand.

Oh, that's pretty, says my mother. What is it?

It's a ship, I say.

I only see blue, says my mother.

It sank, I say.

My mother puts down the drawing.

How was Day One? she asks.

What is Day One? I ask.

Your first day at school! Tomorrow is Day Two!

Do I have to go *again*?

My mother laughs.

Oh, she says, You're such a comic!

The World Screen Headquarters

My first school case was a little rectangular brown chest, inside was a lunchbox, a bottle for cooldrink, a pencil case with coloured pencils and now and then examples of the monstrous art produced by children in Sub A. There was also a thin book with light-blue lines. In this little book Miss Van Wyk pasted notices or wrote short messages to parents. One day after school when my mother and I were in the lounge, I took the book from my school case and gave it to her. Inside was a message: if any new pupils were interested in taking piano lessons, parents should please contact the school office.

Did I read it myself, or did my mother? I have no idea, but let me first tell you about the lounge: my school years took place in the period when this planet's interior decorating reached a low point, when brown and old gold were regarded as beautiful, when thick, sand-coloured carpets and thick brown pottery plates were a middle-class household's pride and joy. This plague hit our homes within two years of the piano message appearing in my school case, but on that day we were still safe, the windows were hung with long white curtains on which a forest of thin black bamboo had been painted, quick brushstrokes like Japanese calligraphy. The furniture had dark-grey seats with light-grey backs, upholstered in a woven fabric with a knobbly texture, underneath were skinny, round, splayed feet made of a light wood. Our lounge looked like a room in which James Bond could listen to a long-playing record and girls with long necks would hold wine glasses, it was sunny, modern and dramatic and I spent as much time there as possible. With our move to the next house this furniture and these curtains vanished; it took me forty years to track down bamboo-patterned fabric again. (Which is now often used as a tablecloth when I entertain with my pitch-black dinner service.)

No discussion of piano lessons was necessary: even when I was little I would swallow hard if I found myself near a thing with keys. In every church, church hall, school hall, dining hall, living room, any place my parents' religion or social circles took us, there would be a musical instrument, battered, out of tune, shabby or beloved. Even the horrible electric home organs that were high fashion in those years tempted me as though they were edible. In Wellington I often went along when Grandfather dropped in on Mr Byleveld, there in the centre of town was the workshop where pianos were rebuilt or repaired, in rows and rows they stood like guards before the vault of melodies; already I'd decided that heaven would one day be filled with pianos, not the harps my mother had read to me about.

An hour after the message had been delivered, my mother crossed the street: three houses down was The World Screen Headquarters.

Here lived Mrs Joubert. She was the town organist, the creator of that vast sound that Sunday after Sunday made my young soul jump for joy, higher and further than any sermon could. In her gloomy dining room an upright piano stood against the wall, crowded with decorative cloths, family members in small frames, glass bowls, porcelain figurines and a few fans from faraway countries. To the left of the piano was a sliding door to the lounge and still further left the arch that led to the big kitchen. The whole house was full of odds and ends, mementos, gifts, cookbooks, reading books, phone books, writing pads, packets of envelopes, pen holders, little bowls with paper clips, postcards, serving platters, glass jars, hard biscuits, fruit, paintings, lamps, crochet work and lace curtains. And screens. Except for the screen door on Uncle Attie and Aunt Miems's back porch, this place surely housed every other screen on earth – there was a screen in front of every window and a screen in front of every door. Screens that could push up, shift, slide out, screens that couldn't move, rolled-up screens that lay underneath the kitchen table and waited for an opening. Here *something* had to be kept in or out.

Like Mrs Joubert, her piano and all her possessions, The World Screen Headquarters didn't attract me or repel me, it didn't welcome me or make me want to flee, it was darker than day and lighter than night, and for some reason I spent a lot of time here, was given food, played outside and explored everything. (Was I by myself? If so, why? Or did my mother visit here that often?) Even today I can close my eyes and remember the whole back garden. The trees – fig trees, lemon trees, mulberry trees, trees without fruit, trees with thin creepers hanging down, trees from which birdcages swung with open doors, with wild branches like creatures dancing too close to one another with arms held high – grew all the way up to the outbuilding with the laundry room, storeroom and garage. Only the garage door didn't have a screen. Rows of neatly laid bricks formed a track to the wide gate. And there was a vine-covered trellis, abundant with grapes that never ripened, beneath which it was always cool and dark, but always also beautiful. Green curls draped themselves lazily over the thin tarred poles.

Here my mother mentioned to Mrs Joubert that we didn't have a piano, but that I was definitely going to take music lessons and that I would have to practise somewhere. Mrs Joubert explained that she had a bit of a lie-down in the back room every afternoon at three on the dot, and that I was welcome to use her piano, it wouldn't disturb her: a dining-room door, a hallway door and a bedroom door lay between her sleep and my talent.

I practised with stupid fingers, three afternoons a week, from three o'clock to four o'clock. Curious and driven, I discovered and memorised my simple phrases, alone in the dusk, thankful for the piano and the biscuits that now and then were left for me, but each time, as in most other places I would visit later in life, completely uncomfortable. Both productive and ill at ease. DIE ONGEMAKLIKE LEWE. THE UNCOMFORTABLE LIFE. The book and song that I always wanted to write, but never would, got its name here.

Then, on a perfectly normal day, I walk into our house, I may have been at school or with The Stoepsusters or with people with food, but I have been away for a few hours. As usual I run to the kitchen. My mother is sitting at the table, my brother is in his high chair. My father stands at the sink. They look different.

What now? I say.

Nothing, says my father.

The newspaper is on the couch, go get it quickly, I want to show you something, my mother says.

I turn around. Something is wrong. I walk to the lounge and look at the couch.

Where is the newspaper? I yell.

Behind you! my father yells.

I turn around. Against the wall is a piano. Dead quiet, bolt up-right, brand new, made of matt wood in the latest fashion, a gallant stool with four curly feet, all here in James Bond's room. I lift the lid and stroke the keys. I don't say thank you, I don't play a note, I don't sit on the stool. I stare. My family stand in the door.

Whose is it? I ask, my voice hoarse.

Yours, you silly child, says my mother.

From Byleveld's store, says my father.

In no other place where we would live as a family would I ever be as happy as in that house with the room with the piano and the bamboo and the sun and the grey jazz furniture. I cannot remember Mrs Joubert's face any more, but every time I think back to The World Screen Headquarters there is another window without a screen, another door standing wide open, even more light. Maybe there never was a single screen, who knows?

It might be different now, but in those days a child definitely did not know what his parents' income was, how much they had to sacrifice for a big moment. And even today a child seldom knows when headquarters appear nearby, when the opportunity to touch the unreachable shows itself, when a portal, disguised as an ornament or instrument, appears.

The Art of Fighting

Was it the answer to my parents' prayers? Was it the trick of an evil fairy or pure coincidence? Japan is very far from Riebeek-Kasteel. But it does indeed happen, a judo instructor is prepared to train the town's sons once a week in an Eastern martial art. We can choose, rugby or judo.

I am almost eight years old and for weeks have felt deeply wronged after the girls at a birthday party were each given a doll with a white dress. These dolls' clothes are made of a special fabric, you can draw patterns and pictures on it and then wash it, and do it again and again! The boys each received a fire engine. I make a hole in the roof of mine and start filling it with coins, I'll buy my own drawing clothes.

We have to play rugby or do judo, I tell my mother.

A judo outfit is very expensive, says my mother.

What does a judo outfit look like? I ask.

Like pyjamas, exactly like white pyjamas, says my mother.

I'm doing judo! I say.

I'm going to colour in those pyjamas, cover them in drawings of dragons, perhaps stick shiny things on them, that is what I decide.

We buy the pyjamas at school, the jacket doesn't have any buttons at all, only a belt. Tuesday afternoon three o'clock we all stand in the hall. There are mats on the floor. We stand in rows, white pyjamas, light-blue belts, we look like dwarfs in a storybook with only one colour. The instructor is young and friendly, he doesn't look as grumpy as the other teachers who coach sports. He tells us that he gives judo lessons every afternoon in another town, it's a privilege for him, judo makes the world tolerant and safe.

Judo consists of sudden decisions and movement, he says, We don't attack, we defend.

This gives me confidence. I raise my hand.

Can I make my belt green or pink?

Some of the boys snort.

In judo we have levels, you don't colour your belt, you earn it, says the instructor. My heart sinks to the floor, old and young, they all disappoint you, nothing is what it should be, nobody is tolerant, nothing is safe. But it is better than rugby.

Before we can fight, we each have to pick a friend, I pick Gideon. He has a soft face like me and also cries at athletics. The instructor explains grips and throws. And that it is important to know how to fall. One must throw and the other one must fall. Gideon hesitantly grabs at my belt. My jacket falls open.

Don't, I say.

I lay myself down and Gideon lies on top of me. Later I lie on top. When the judo instructor comes closer, we pull a bit on each other's clothes. Judo is not so bad. I just don't know how they will ever decide who is attacking and who is defending.

On a very warm Tuesday afternoon I walk home after another judo class. I'm annoyed because of the heat and because of my clothes and belt that never change colour. I want a vienna at the corner shop, but a judo outfit doesn't have pockets and so I don't have 5c with me.

You! Pudding face! a voice says.

I look around. Right behind me is Fudge. (He was a tall child who looked as if he spent every day by the sea, tanned with policeman muscles, brush-cut hair and orange eyebrows. Everyone knew he looked for trouble with children and was friendly to grown-ups. He was bigger than any of the children in school, perhaps he was stupid, but nobody asked.) He's never spoken to me before. Why now? What's happening? I look straight ahead.

You! Doll-boy! he says.

I hear all the menace and all the flames of hell in his voice. I feel hot behind my neck, over my whole head. And ice-cold behind my legs, I am shaking like a little machine, it will never, ever stop again, this is how a child changes into a ghost.

Butterfly! I am going to hurt you! he says, now much closer.

Die, pig, die, I say softly, my dry lips clinging helplessly to each other. I had heard it a few months before at the church camp when two cleaners had a fist fight behind the dustbins, die, pig, die. I had put it away and say it now.

There is a sudden whoosh, like the wing of an eagle. Aunt Gagiano stops next to me with her massive Peugeot.

I know you're just a stone's throw from home, but get in before you melt in this sun, she laughs.

I get in. And I shiver like after a bath in winter.

Don't pay attention to that Fudge child, he's just hot air, the Lord gives and the Lord takes away, says Aunt Gagiano.

She stops in front of her home.

Do you want to come inside for orange juice? she asks.

No, thank you, I shiver.

It is only the empty yard next to her house and then it's our house. Twenty child's steps, but it takes me a hundred long years before

I push open our gate. Not once do I look behind me. I am a little ghost, forward, forward.

I never saw him again. Two weeks later, just before first break, the school principal came to our class and explained in a soft voice that Fudge wouldn't be coming back to our school, he'd had an accident the day before, he'd been on his bicycle on the Bothmaskloof pass. The principal said it was good to be sad and if anybody wanted to go home, they were welcome to do so.

I went to sit on a low wall outside and opened my lunchbox. Inside was brown bread with peanut butter. I couldn't believe it, my mother knew I didn't eat peanut butter, I don't eat it, I don't eat it. But she still didn't stop, once a week it was in my lunchbox. I couldn't believe it.

Luxurious

Technically I am still little, only three years out of toddlerhood. I am unsatisfied and uncomfortable, but I assume everything will be explained to me at some later point, so I keep quiet as much as possible, I wait like a good boy to be told how things work. All I want to do is round up everyone in town and yell, hysterically and uncontrollably, Right! It's time! Tell me what is going on! This is wrong! What are you hiding? Why is this lasting so long?

What lasts too long is my darkness and my heaviness. Already I can describe the hours of my day to every rock in the front garden and every reed out back by the failing vlei. Ordinary. Ordinary. Bad. Bad. Very bad. Breathless. Suspicious. Better. Ordinary. Almost good. Bad again. Very, very bad. Dead as a dodo. Still alive. Slightly better. Sleep.

ALMOST GOOD is therefore the best time of my day, that's how well I'm doing. GOOD or VERY GOOD is only at Grandmother's house, not here. So I have to explain to myself: I cannot do what other children do, they are lighter and do not have a Big Grey. The Big

Grey lives in my schoolbag. (Where else? The heaviness begins every morning when I pick up my bag, Saturdays are lighter, Sundays the grey starts to pile up again.) What the Big Grey looks like when it is in the darkness of my bag, I don't know. As soon as I start walking, my bag shakes, the Big Grey finds little holes and starts to leak outside. Like a poisonous fog it hangs around me, then starts to form corners until the gloom is square like a big cardboard box that leaves only my head and feet uncovered. This box becomes heavier and lighter, bigger and smaller, it makes me walk slower, get stuck in doors, stumble over stairs, bump against walls, it makes my fingers stupid near the piano, makes sure that I never learn how to hug or embrace someone, never, ever run into someone's arms. I know it's not my imagination, I can hear them whispering – certain walls, the empty house on the corner where the tar ends, the gateposts in front of the church: Here comes the heavy child! Shh, he has his darkness with him!

I tell myself a time will come when a being, gigantic and vivid, possibly clad like many heroes in metal, fleet of foot and very clever, will appear, faster than a falcon. He will grab the Big Grey with a sweep of his arm and take it to the penal colony where all grey must live.

This being does appear, waiting in the hallway one afternoon after school, dressed in a brown pinafore with a mustard-yellow cardigan. It is my mother. In her hand is a roll of bright paper with a sheet of brown paper around it. She holds it towards me. My name and our address are typed on the brown paper.

What is it? I ask.

It's the magazine we saw in the *Huisgenoot*, my mother says, Don't you remember? Your father said we could order it.

Carefully I remove the brown paper, careful, careful, I'm going to save it. I roll the magazine open. There is a soft noise and the fern in the hallway shivers, it is the flight of the Big Grey, first to the front door and then back into my bag.

This is not like when the piano appeared, that moment was a step into a new doorway; this thing I am holding now is a luxury. We live simply; something with your name on, something that is delivered so your grey can flee, is almost unreal.

Bollie was a magazine for children, full of comic strips, among others the adventures of a hare family with Bollie the leading character. I devour every word and picture, afterwards I cannot remember even one story, my joy is the paper, the colours, the way Bollie and his life are drawn, the way the ink shines on the pages, the way the paper rustles, the way something smells when it is brand new, when it was packaged before it could lie on a shop's shelf or be handled without care.

Again and again *Bollie* was delivered, a whole afternoon and a whole evening without grey. I treasured it like jewellery, hid it before my little brother could damage it, paged through it again and again, imagined myself living in a place where dining tables looked like those of the brightly dressed hare family, where puddings and cakes were as big as the guests, where raisins spilled out of loaves of bread and steam rose from mugs of hot chocolate. Even today my family still uses it as an adjective: Bollie book biscuits, Bollie book bread, Bollie book towers.

Later there were more magazines, *Patrys, Tina, Panorama*. *Patrys* was full of activities, facts and things you could cut out; it would break my heart to cut up one of my treasures, I only cut out things when my mother was done with *her* magazines. *Tina* was exclusively for teenage girls and for me, how it ended up in our home, how my father allowed it, I do not know. *Panorama* was a big magazine with expensive paper, full-page photos of nature – in which I had no interest at all – and articles in a language that could not appeal to any child, but it was delivered in a big envelope without any folds and it smelled of promise, new and mysterious. I handled it as though it was a message from a far-off place, a document for the nobility.

The Big Grey would always stay with me, and later I would become smarter and think up many escapes, but in that little town of my early school-going years and countless realisations, paper was my first luxury and constant salvation. On magazine days the stones and reeds knew, here it is VERY GOOD.

Paper is the bringer of messages, the shepherd of the earth's biggest stories, the proof of artists' immortality, somewhere homes are made of it, everywhere food is eaten from it, somewhere it is worn as clothing, it brings birthday wishes and Christmas greetings, it fans people cool, it is proof that you passed, it wraps presents.

After the first magazines many envelopes followed. I floated when I excelled, yelled when I won something, got a fright when I disappointed, was disgusted when I got my first call-up papers for the army. Later there were cruel papers, rejections of love, poisonous newspaper reviews, reminders of student debts.

But at first there was only joy. And then, soon after the first *Bollie*, my father's and my life changed.

It is my birthday. My mother bakes a cake, it is a chocolate loco-motive, I can't believe my eyes, how did Mother make this whole thing? Grandfather and Grandmother come from Wellington. It is one of the best days ever. Friends appear. Who invited them? (A little grey escapes from my bag.) Mother puts down the cake and everyone sings. I want to eat the chimney. I break it off, it is an empty toilet roll with icing. (More grey.) I decide to eat the cab. It is an empty tissue box. (Lots of grey!) Eventually there is something to eat, the chocolate roll in the middle, but I don't feel like it any more. My father gives me my present, it's a rugby ball, brand new and light brown, leather or plastic, I close my eyes and make a wish, I open my eyes, it isn't an Easter egg, still a ball. I put it aside. Grandmother gives me her present. It is wrapped in Christmas paper. (The grey becomes less.) I open it. It is a paper doll, a girl with sheets and sheets of clothes you can cut out, short strips wrap around her body and make the clothes stick. She can be a princess, a teacher, a policewoman, a lady with her own shop.

One thing about Grandmother – she could shop like no one else. She often dragged big brown paper bags into her kitchen and began to unpack. Twenty boxes of canary seed. Thirty boxes of cough mixture. Forty packages of orange hair dye.

Grandfather: What are you doing with the seed? Who has budgies?

Grandmother: It was on sale, it would be stupid to leave such a bargain behind.

Grandfather: And the cough mixture? Who is coughing?

Grandmother: You! Soon!

Grandfather: No, heavens, Grandmother, and the hair dye?

Grandmother: Ben, that pharmacy is closing, the things are marked down, if the wrong woman gets hold of it she'll make a fool of herself, I had to take it.

Grandmother had definitely been in a shop somewhere, maybe stood with a small truck or a set of blocks in her hand and then saw the paper dolls were much cheaper. That's all. But it shifts my reality as quickly as someone taking a pair of scissors from a drawer. My princess changes her appearance within minutes, she moves between worlds. My friends disappear, Grandmother and Grandfather go home, Mother does the dishes, Father gives my brother a bath, I am in my room, the door is closed, the grey is gone, I am cutting out a blouse. I do not dream of a braid down my back or a dress on my body, I do not want to be a girl, but I have a job to do. I dress my princess and I listen to her speak, she says the strangest thing: One day you can change your clothes just as quickly.

When? I ask.

My father opens the door. I do not look up. He opens the cupboard and puts the rugby ball next to my shoes. He says nothing, he merely closes the door behind him. And he would do it again, every time I broke his heart.

A Table for Prentjie

Somewhere near the church, the main road's tar disappeared and there, where gravel became ground, they sat in a row: church, school, tennis courts, dormitory. In this dormitory my mother worked a few times a week, she had to supervise until the sun began to set. On these days I had to stay there after school; I have no idea where my baby brother was.

A few years ago I visited the town for the first time since I left there at the age of nine. I was invited to do a show at the church hall; this hall had been a gigantic building where all of the town's plans began or ended, but when I went back I was shocked to see how small and cramped the hall actually was. This has happened a few times: childhood buildings that had shrunk so much over the years that on a return visit they were invariably unrecognisable and always bitterly disappointing. This would also be the case with the dormitory, but for the purposes of this story I have kept it in its original form, long, pale and damning.

The occupants were farm children – the descendants of both wealthy and struggling farmers – who all went back home on Friday afternoons, city children who'd been sent there to keep out of trouble, and a few town children from families too miserable to have any future prospects. A few had to stay there over weekends and even holidays. And when my mother was on duty, I wandered about, one afternoon after another.

The youngest children played outside, the rest had to do their homework in the dining hall. I was too young for real homework and so I wandered. The front door opened onto a small entrance hall and then you could turn left or right down a long corridor with pale, polished floors and on both sides a multitude of doors. There was a forgotten lounge, an office, bedrooms for staff, single rooms and dorm rooms for pupils (I don't know how it was decided who would sleep in a dorm room and who in a single room), bathrooms and the dining hall. At the end of the corridor, on either side there were sharp turns to even more rooms and the long wing at the back that consisted of laundry rooms, storerooms and the kitchen; from above thus a perfect 8.

Here there was no pleasure – perhaps for others, but I couldn't find anything, not a single pretty thing, no mysterious corners or dancing shadows, only empty walls, rooms and children. And The Smell. There was an inescapable smell that would not budge for even a moment – not the smell of the cleaning products that are still so popular in shiny corridors, nor that of chicken pie baking in big ovens, nor that of coffee escaping from a staffroom; it was a dead smell, a grim grey smell. Mother was terribly upset when I once began sniffing a slice of bread in front of the other children, I couldn't help it, I was certain The Smell hid in the thick slices of death's bread that were slapped down each day in front of everyone. No butter or jam could disguise those dreary sponges.

Maybe it was the recipes of those years, or the fact that not every town had someone like my grandmother, but only tiredness and drabness ever came out of that big kitchen. I wanted to scream, Where are the rusks, where are the scones, where are our biscuits, we are little children! That was where I first had The Horrors, when trays with plastic containers filled with quicksand and funeral sludge were carried into the dining hall. I would wait until my mother looked away and then disappear down the corridor.

It was during one of these furious I-have-the-horrors-and-I-am-hungry strolls that I saw the door to a boy's room was wide open. He was sitting on his bed and paging through a book. His feet were off the ground. I never knew his name, in my thoughts I called him Prentjie. He was the oldest child in the dormitory, but also the smallest; he was quiet and very beautiful, it looked as though he'd been drawn, his clothes were never dirty or wrinkled, not a single blond hair was ever out of place, he never looked for trouble and only spoke when someone asked him a question. All the children in the world should be like him. I liked him a lot.

I stood and looked at Prentjie in his barren room, not for so long that he would notice, but long enough to see there was nothing beautiful, not a rug, not a chair, only a bed and a wardrobe with a suitcase on top; the walls were empty, the only picture was Prentjie. Why wasn't he with the others in the dining hall? Was he also escaping from The Smell? And where would he go? He only had his ugly room, I felt so sorry for him, for days I wondered what I would do if I had to live in a room without any of my things.

It was a weekday afternoon, warm, a few children played listlessly next to the dormitory, the rest sat staring at their books in the dining hall. I was in the corridor. Prentjie's bedroom door was open. I walked closer to see. He and his book were not on the bed. But the Yellow Juffrou was on her knees next to the bed. She was one of the teachers who lived in the dormitory, youngish with short, light-yellow hair and an unusually broad face, with a dimple in each cheek that made her look like she was constantly smiling. She was the Standard Two teacher and wore a yellow cardigan every day.

In her hand was a pencil. She drew a thin horizontal line on the wall, then another one directly below the first, and connected the two at both ends. Then she drew two thin lines from the left-hand corner to the floor, and the same on the right-hand side: a table!

My mother appeared in the corridor.

Are you coming? she asked.

Her handbag hung from one arm, my brother from the other. He recognised me and laughed with an open mouth, he bent his knees and jumped up and down with his short little legs. Go home, play noisily until dinner, bath until the whole floor was under water, that's what he waited for on dormitory days. But I didn't feel like playing. Something was happening. What was the Yellow Juffrou doing? I knew sleep helped children grow, but I was awake the whole night.

The next day school took hours, just finish now! I stormed down the stairs, past the tennis courts, in through the dormitory's front door, came to a stop in the entrance hall and panted, waiting for all the children to disappear into the dining hall for lunch and The Smell. I prayed Prentjie's door would be open.

Finally. The corridor was empty. Prentjie's door was open. Next to his bed, exactly where it had been drawn, was a table. I gasped. That was why he had his own room! That was why he was so small! That was why he didn't speak! There was magic happening here, it was a chosen room!

But why only the table? Why not a chair? Was the Yellow Juffrou worried she would get caught? I opened my school case, I grabbed a pencil. The children didn't eat for long, afterwards they went to their rooms to change and play before homework. Whatever was going on here, I was still sorry for Prentjie. Next to the table I drew him a chair, I drew quickly and the feet were skew, but the magic would fix them. I also drew him paintings against the wall, storybooks in a row, an extra window that overlooked a river with fish and small boats, a big potplant with finger leaves like the one on our porch, a tin of biscuits, another tin of rusks, a radio, a standing lamp, two fat cats and a bicycle. It would be a glorious room; after this Prentjie would be my friend.

Your mother is going to kill you, a voice said.

I jerked around. One of the kitchen ladies was standing in the doorway. She was the one who always sliced and stacked the smelly bread.

Who scribbles on a wall? she asked.

The Yellow Juffrou, I said.

Your mother will kill you twice, you can't say the Yellow Juffrou!

She drew the table, and then the room made it real! I'm only drawing little things, he has nothing!

She only marked where the table should go, as an example, so the workers would know where, all the older children are getting desks next to their beds!

No!

I sobbed out loud. The kitchen lady twitched her nose.

Don't cry, she said, They'll hear you. We'll get a cloth and quickly clean this up.

She turned around and disappeared.

I cried from fright and because there weren't any miracles and because of being killed twice. And because of Prentjie who only had a table. Two kitchen ladies appeared. Each with a big cloth and a spray bottle. The first one put her hand on my head.

Go wash your face, we won't tell a soul, she said.

I walked down the hall. I could hear them talk.

What happened here? asked the one.

The funny one wanted to do magic, said the other. His poor, poor mother.

Church Camp, Beef Mince, Nero

I sit in the back of the car. Next to me is my baby brother in his car seat, a primitive contraption of metal, canvas and leather, a grotesque garden chair minus the feet. My mother sits in front with a basket on her lap. At the back of the car my father is putting the last of the set of blue suitcases in the boot. He gets in the car and turns the key. We reverse into the street, my father pulls the hand brake, it goes kkrrr! like when the dog bites through a bone. My father gets out, closes the gate and gets back in the car. We drive past the small vineyard, up the hill, past The Stoepsusters' house, and turn right. My stomach feels hollow, the anxiety mouse starts gnawing at me. For nice things – Grandmother's Wellington, shopping trips, Johannesburg's Cape (that's what Grandfather called Paarl) – we always turn left.

Where are we going? I ask.

We're on our way to the church camp, says my mother.

Where is it? I ask.

A little bit further, says my father.

What are we going to do there? I ask.

We're going to visit, says my father.

And sing, says my mother. We're going to read the Bible, tell you children stories, we're going to hold hands and dance in circles. And we are going to pray a lot.

But we can pray at home too, I say.

Sometimes a person needs to go away for a little while, says my mother. You need to be with people who think and believe like you do, you need silence so you can concentrate.

Krst, krst, gnaws the mouse.

But we can concentrate at home, I say.

Sometimes children need to talk less and just be obedient, says my father.

He turns left up a narrow street, stops before a metal gate, winds down his window and waves his arm. Someone pushes open the gate and we drive inside and park in a carport. There are lots of cars, rows and rows of them in parallel.

Here we are, says my father, Let's go look for our rondavel.

Our home was at the upper end of Riebeek-Kasteel, the church camp was right in the middle of Riebeek West. The distance between the two was six kilometres. My parents had packed every suitcase we owned, strapped my little brother to an insect and woken my anxiety mouse so we could drive less than ten minutes to dance in circles and to concentrate.

My father opens the boot.

Rugby ball, soccer ball, beach ball, I brought them all, he says, There are lots of children here and plenty of space, you can play until you get tired.

Those were the last words I heard. After that I saw mouths moving, saw eyes blink, saw the sun rise and set, saw people scurry about, saw hands playing the guitar, saw matches light lanterns and saw blankets cover mothers and their babies. There was a row of mini-buildings with pointy roofs; cement, asbestos, corrugated iron, wood, cardboard, who knew what had been used to manufacture these human holders, who knew why my father called them rondavels. There were a few trees in a big open area with poor grass (my one uncle's first wife always put on her sunglasses in the fear that she would have to drive past poor grass. Hate it! she sighed. Apparently this was the result when a lawn got just enough water not to die, but too little to be properly green), a hall where gatherings took place, a side veranda where meals were served at long tables, and next door a square building that consisted of a storeroom and a big kitchen. Where these two buildings met there was a square, dark and out of sight, with rubbish bins and crates and gardening equipment. I came to have a look every day. At some stage one of the world's big and invisible rulers, Perversion, gives every child an invisible little helper that leads him to places and situations where improprieties – naughty things – might take place. It was here that, on the last day, when the expectation of going back home gradually restored my hearing, I saw two workers having a fist fight and one hissed the deadly command, Die, pig, die.

One ray of light during my time at the camp: there was beef mince, lots of beef mince. Bobotie, shepherd's pie, sausage, meatballs, round and rectangular meat pies, spaghetti with mince and tomato, mince with fried onions and grated cheese . . . I was amazed at the big metal containers, the amounts, the smell. The only big amounts in my life were the dormitory slop and the stench of it. Here it was almost festive. Three meals a day appeared from the big camp kitchen, also tea in the morning and warm milk at night. Each of these five helpings was supplemented with bread. Toast, sandwiches, thick slices of fresh bread lined up on trays, bread soldiers dipped in egg and grilled, also bread pudding. I only knew two kinds of bread: shop bread, white, brown or wholegrain, soft and ordinary; and farm bread, crunchy crust on the outside, solid and snow white on the inside. The bread in the camp was different: big slices, good enough to eat without butter, looked home-baked, but delivered twice a day at the big metal gate. I called it prayer bread. And encountered it only afterwards, more than ten years later when I again attended a church camp, I was in love with a vision of a youth worker and had heard there were open showers on the grounds.

Back to Riebeek West: On the second-last evening everyone sits in the hall, on chairs, crates, cushions and laps; a white cloth has been strung against the wall up front, at the back is a film projector on a high table. Someone turns off the lights and monsters begin to jump around on the white cloth. A few people turn around but then the movie starts behaving.

A grey city appears, full of pillars, massive buildings, women with braided hair, men in long garments, soldiers with swords, horses, coaches without roofs and markets where live animals are peddled.

It's Rome, my mother mouths.

Is it near Wellington? I ask.

No, my mother's mouth explains, It's overseas, hundreds of years ago.

A man has golden leaves on his head. Red fabric hangs from his shoulder and a white cloak drags behind him. (I now know that the actor was Peter Ustinov.) He is furious, he walks up and down in a marble hall, he balls his fists and yells at a row of anxious people, I hear nothing.

Emperor Nero, explains my father's mouth.

The mouse is awake and eats at me. At once the whole cloth is full of people, thousands, they sit in rows in a big round place. This is the most people I have ever seen, also the biggest place, a roofless church, a tent-less circus, a treeless athletics day. The mouse is suddenly quiet, both of us know big trouble is coming.

In the middle of the crowd is an empty circle. Small groups of people begin to appear, they look scared and hold on to each other.

The Christians, explains my mother's mouth.

Nero lifts his fist and then jerks it downwards.

Rubbish! That is all my father's mouth forms.

Inside a thick wall a barred gate is raised and one lion after another slinks into my young life. Their big paws slash at the Christians, the thousands of people jump up and shake their fists in the air, Nero smiles broadly, a thin woman next to him feasts on a bunch of grapes. Against a cloth in Riebeek West: lunacy. I can't hear myself, but I know I'm crying, on my mother's lap my baby brother wakes up and looks at me, he smiles, a lion rips off someone's arm, my father picks me up and carries me outside, a strange woman brings me sugar water.

A few months later we visited Grandmother. One afternoon we drove to Paarl to see a movie. There was a theatre close to the Tower Church, unlike at the drive-ins we sat very close to the screen, like the lions at the church camp everything was too big and too close. The movie was *Hawaii*, an odd story with Julie Andrews in the lead role; it had come out three years earlier, but was shown on that day in Paarl.

Julie Andrews and a bunch of English people in uniforms sailed in an old-fashioned ship on a rough sea. There they met the queen or leader of the island. She was a giantess, she was fascinated with the ship and wanted to see the inside. Because she was too big to climb the ladder at the side, a primitive crane had to be built. Unlike at the church camp, all my senses were fully functional and I could hear everything. Were the waves too rough? Was the music too dramatic? By the time the unwieldy body started swinging to and fro above the ship, things became just too much. I cried ferociously, possibly screamed, I was amazed (and a little impressed) by my volume, but I couldn't stop. Again my father had to carry me out, again I was soothed with food.

Until then the universe had consisted of Riebeek-Kasteel, Riebeek West, Wellington and Paarl. Rome and Hawaii were unthinkable; that people could think up such things, so cruel and on such a scale and without warning, was unthinkable, that each time after such a disillusionment we could drive back home like nothing was wrong, it was unthinkable. Overwhelming, inconceivable, impossible.

War

Whether we drove directly from home, or we first went to Wellington, or my little brother was dropped off somewhere, or I was wearing a hat or not, details like these were all erased by my second emergency coma. Only the very worst moments, the life-threatening images, the most barbaric sounds, those remained. We must have parked somewhere, we must have walked far, my father would have held my hand, perhaps a blanket under his arm, my mother would have carried a bag or a basket, at some point we would have stood in a queue, bought tickets, sucked on orange ice lollies.

The experience starts suddenly, explodes like a surprising scene – smell, temperature, sound, movement, feeling, everything at once. I must have been wearing sandals, my feet are white from the dust and it is more than just seeing, I can feel it, dry, dry, dry. Hard soil with light powder that puffs round your ankles, trampled grass, straw-like and sharp, it stabs between my open toes like knives. For some reason I am smaller than usual, short and close to the ground, I reach up, up, but I stay down. I see dusty shoes, men and women all in the same shoes, some shoes are brown, now sandy from the dust, some shoes are black, now grey from the dust. All shoes are visible, trouser legs end at the ankle, dresses' hems and petticoat ruffles too.

The dresses: Each a wide, flared skirt, with narrow pleats going up to the waist, shapeless bodice, puffy sleeves with bows on the elbows. The colours are dull, light pink, light blue, light yellow, light green. Nobody stands still, the dresses are in a hurry, definitely on their way to an event, everyone is called. I am too short, I cannot see the world, the dresses ball around me, I am an ant on a bazaar table, surrounded by sponge cakes, a big finger is going to squash me any minute. I jerk myself higher, I see their shoulders, white cloths hang like on the backs of armchairs. I jerk myself again, even higher, there are no faces, no hair, only bonnets, white things that first bulge like the heads of the octopuses in my picture book, then point to the front. At the back pleated flaps hang like in the windows of The Earth Houses.

I know my parents are on either side of me, but I don't look at them, I stagger through the chaos like a wind-up duck, bent over like our town's fat men walking at night, can't go on, dare not stop, can't go on, dare not stop.

Where are we? I call.

This is the Goodwood Showgrounds, says my mother, It's the big Republic festival.

We have to go! I yell.

What are you talking about? says my mother, We haven't even found a spot yet!

What are these people doing? I yell.

They're dancing in front, says my mother, Look at that! Heavens, did you know so many people could make circles?!

In front of us appears a field bigger than the church, the school and the dormitory grounds combined. There are people who have formed circles and are now holding one another's hands. Man, woman, man, woman, the men are wearing waistcoats, blue or orange. Waistcoat, puff cake, waistcoat, puff cake, thirty or forty in a circle, thirty or forty circles in an empty space. All the circles are moving in circles, it's pretty. Ugly makes pretty. But the pretty is only the circling of the circles, not the bonnets, also not the waistcoats, also not the shoes and DEFINITELY not the sounds. Ugly makes ugly. They sing. The whole lot sings. It is a cheerful melody, they sing with enthusiasm, but like all outdoor singing it disappears immediately. There are musical instruments, a big platform serves as a stage; fabrics, orange, white and blue, span the carcass. On top there is an upright piano played by a woman in a bonnet, there is a half-moon of men with guitars and accordions and a wild bear with a cloth hat behind a set of drums, I recognise all the instruments. Right in front is a man with pitch-black hair and a bow-tie, he raises a silver bellows and pulls it open and closed like when Grandfather gets the fire going. The bellows screams murder, The Vuurhoutjies are torturing a cat or chasing a piglet.

It's called folk dancing, says my mother.

And those are the last words of the day.

I see how my father throws open the blanket, how my mother sits down and takes a tupperware container from the basket. We are going to stay here for a long time, in this flat hell. Nero is suddenly there, life-sized between two accordions, he lifts his fist and jerks it down. The gates lift and the lions storm. They devour the man with the bow-tie and bellows first. Blood on the bonnets, blood on the shoes. Thump, thump, hammer my ears. And then all sound is gone. It is quiet again. Like in Riebeek West it is a throng of people, open mouths, hand gestures, crowds in the arena, crowds looking on, I hear nothing.

The next Saturday my mother carries her basket out the front door.

Come, she says, Go wash your hands so we can go. And take some of your books so you have something to do.

Where are we going now? I ask.

We're going to braai! says my mother, I told you already. And fetch your brother's red blanket, he'll be asleep before we eat.

I'll get the blanket, but I'm not going!

What did you say?

I'm not going, I hate those people.

Since when do we talk like that? Where did you learn that word?

Their house is ugly and they say stupid things.

Eben! calls my mother.

My father appears from the garage.

Someone has decided he's not going, says my mother.

My father looks at me.

Are you going to get in yourself or do I have to come and fetch you?

I go up the stairs, walk into the house, do not wash my hands, grab the red blanket and get in the car. Five minutes later we stop at the house with the forget-me faces. My baby brother jumps out and runs to the swing behind the trailers. The people come out to greet us, the woman looks at me.

Isn't he getting out?

No, dear, says my mother, He's full of nonsense again.

Enjoy the wait! says the woman.

Stupid thing.

I lie on the back seat, the hours feel like weeks. If they keep on taking me to places I don't want to be, I'll show them. There in the back of the car I declare war. I don't know yet that it will be a fifteen-year war, but I have begun to learn that the decisions I make when I am furious are my best, then nothing makes me change my mind. So I lie down until my legs go numb. Once my father comes to look. I lie with my eyes closed. Later my mother opens the door.

Here are some choppies, she says, And that thin sausage you like so much. And braaibrood. And foam pudding. With custard. Come, eat quickly.

I pretend to sleep. My mother leaves. Later I do fall asleep and only wake up when my father lifts me up and carries me inside. My stomach aches from hunger. I feel terribly sorry for myself, but I won't cry, or eat, or talk. It's war.

Eucalyptus

My first original stage concoctions already began drawing attention at university. I was always running between the Conserv-
atory's concert hall, the HB Thom theatre and the newly built
amphitheatre next to the library, panting and feverish, always
busy with a one-man show or an opera or a pop oratory, seldom
in the lecture hall where I was supposed to be. In my third year
a group of actors from Cape Town knocked on my door, I wrote
music for a play and my years at the provincial arts council began.
There were revues and dramas and things nobody could explain
(always called cabarets!), I accompanied, wrote, adapted, every
now and then sang a few notes from the corner. As an accompanist
or orchestra member I toured the entire country and got to know
every theatre.

But I wanted to sing solos, in the centre of the stage, draped in
outfits dreamt up in reveries of faraway places, arms stretched out
like an emperor, that was after all what I'd done at university, had
everyone forgotten? I delivered photographs, cassettes, gifts and
files of my life story to every newspaper, magazine, record com-

pany, studio, nightclub, jazz club, theatre and impresario. Obscure, they said. The image is wrong. The sound is experimental. The voice is completely impossible. What is going on with the lyrics? I was devastated and ready for a fight at the same time, I smoked myself hoarse, cried myself even hoarser and kept selling; there was no back-up plan. Eventually it was the arts councils that took a chance again. Soon the shows began selling out, countrywide tours were offered, again and again. Magazines began to notice, the first cover stories began to appear (there were complaints!), television programmes couldn't get enough (there were even more complaints!), tongues were wagging, my tears disappeared as money appeared.

And so, bit by bit, after ten years on the stage, I stopped wondering how long it would take. The phone and fax cooed, two, three, even four new productions a year were offered, less and less often by me; I could name my price, I was the darling of the box office. The platteland stifled its fears and started calling, town after town begged for a visit. I began to travel, driving across plains and over hills, on my own or with an accompanist or with a band. Halls were decorated, flowers were carted over, I was welcomed with baked goods and bags of loose banknotes.

Bit by bit sleep forsook me, not because of my schedule or my carousing; because a constant anxiety came and sat on my chest, a burning stomach was my new travelling companion, I was nauseous before and after every meal, the fear that so often took hold of me at school and university was now with me all the time. My body's malfunctioning because of the environment, a condition that would become so bad twenty years on that consulting rooms and hospitals were a regular destination, found its roots here.

One Tuesday I am lying on the bed against the wall in my rescuer's office. Dr Steenkamp is a beautiful man with a beautiful heart, a beautiful voice and the healthiest mind I will ever know. His office is up the stairs, through the window you look at the crown of a great, watchful tree, there is no better place.

He asks me if I can feel the fear.

I explain that it is pressing on my chest and my stomach, also around my head, like a band that keeps on tightening itself.

He asks if there are times when it is worse than usual.

I answer that it's on those days when I have to give a show in a small town, also the day before.

He asks me what happens on a day like that.

I answer that the closer I get to the town the more afraid I become, that my mouth dries up, that I get headaches, that I become sad and want to go far away.

He asks if something bad or ugly happens in these towns, if I'm threatened or insulted.

I shake my head, the people are always very excited and welcoming.

He asks if there is an image in my mind, something that is the same in every town, something that will appear the moment I think about such a town.

I say there is always an avenue of trees as you enter a town, a row on each side of the road.

Dr Steenkamp asks if it is pretty or ugly.

I answer that it is pretty, always very pretty.

He says I must close my eyes, breathe normally, allow the pressure around my head and on my chest and stomach to become worse or better, see if the avenue of trees changes in my mind, if something happens.

I am in Riebeek-Kasteel, seven or eight years old, it is very hot. And dry. I am barefoot. I am wearing a vest and my hated white shorts. I walk past the church hall, past the house where we always visit, the people with the forget-me faces, no one will ever know who they are, we just visit them a lot, the man struggles with his businesses, my father often tries to help, there are three trailers, all their tyres are flat. I carry on straight, tar becomes dirt, becomes tar again, becomes dirt again. The town lies behind me, here and there are houses, like beggars' teeth, ahead of me are the trees, two rows of eucalyptus, tall and grey, close to the ground their bark has split open and broken away, the trunks are stained and cling with open toes to the parched earth, I shudder and think of chicken's feet that convulse after the slaughter in Aunt Stienie's yard.

I walk through the trees and hear the first children. There are two gateposts without a gate, inside awaits our athletics track. That's what everyone calls it, but it's just an open piece of land, barren, covered in all the dust the Devil had left over after he had made hell, all of it strewn here. And here, in this dust, every child who doesn't know that the Devil made sin too is going to run yelling and laughing between two chalk lines, squatting and waiting for a teacher to shout at them or shoot a pistol in the air. Some only run for a bit and then get a pat on the back, others run further, a whole circle, others run with a stick they pass to another one waiting, sometimes a child is raised on shoulders while others clap.

What am I doing? I'm unsure, my head is a whirlwind of smiles, whistles, fold-up chairs and floppy hats, round and round and round, around me there is a confusion of bodies and flags. I recognise a classmate and see he has a can of cooldrink in his hand. Another one is eating a pie. That means the grown-ups have arrived. Has time passed? Aren't we practising any more? Is it athletics day? How many times have I walked through the trees? A hand on my shoulder pushes me towards a row of children. A shot goes off, I run, wildly and without getting anywhere, furious and miserable. Someone, the Devil's helper, yells through a megaphone. Afterwards I walk between the cars, there are more eucalyptus, not in rows but in clusters like they're gossiping about someone, there are small tents with tables, I see my mother, she is wearing sunglasses and holding my little brother, my father is standing next to a pole with flags, he and the other men laugh with their heads thrown back. My father was a teller of jokes, and he would tell his athletics joke for the rest of his life: No, little Niël ran so hard that no one was behind him!

I walk home, my feet completely covered in dust, top and bottom, up to my ankles; my soles are rough paper. I feel sick.

Dr Steenkamp lets me lie until all the pressure is gone. The band around my head is gone. I open my eyes. Slowly I get up from the bed. For the first time in nearly thirty years I am free of dust and athletics.

Trees are the landmarks of my physical existence. My home of the past seventeen years is in the middle of a garden with so many trees it's practically a forest. The road to my home is a tree-shaded lane where the branches reach across from both sides and meet in the middle in a solid arc. Kings. Even Riebeek-Kasteel, at the upper end of the town, was a paradise of trees, both wild and in orchards, that stretched up into the folds of the mountains and all the way to Riebeek West, luxuriant and dark, like the wig of a stately woman, as she waits in riches and cool shade. In contrast, in the lower part of the town, which was empty and neglected, there were eucalyptus in two short rows, like the pubis of a whore left vulnerable and exhausted while those without thought go their dusty way.

Nowadays the eucalyptus is described as alien, unwelcome. Heavens, I have to defend every tree, what is more alien than me? Let them be, let them steal water, let them tower above everything, they live without choosing, someone else's history has put them there.

Attie and Miems

Here was a yard with life. And a home with its own laws, no sign of the town culture. Welcome to the edge of the world.

You reached Uncle Attie and Aunt Miems's property by driving straight through the town right to the lower end, turning left onto the last street, then right at the second gate; this big gate was always open, chickens and dogs saw something humans couldn't, they would sprint right up to the friendly gap and then simply turn around, never setting foot in the street. There was a second gate, the small one that led to the front door, but that was for people in jackets, the minister, policeman, undertaker, postman.

In through the gate: the yard was big, parched and hard as nails. Here twenty cars could park, one hundred people could dance or twelve horses could be saddled. To the right was a long building with a corrugated-iron roof and many doors – I used to think Uncle Attie had his own village with its own high street and businesses. There was parking for their car, there was a workshop, another one, storerooms, the world's only zoo with an open door, a space with bicycles and wheelbarrows and an honorary spot for the school bus.

To the left of the yard was the house, the same length as Uncle Attie's own high street. You walked round the corner, past the kitchen window, past the low porch wall to the step. One step and you were on the porch. To the left was the screen door to the kitchen, to the right was the screen door to the laundry room. (Yes, there were two screen doors in Riebeek-Kasteel that Mrs Joubert couldn't get her hands on!)

In at the left-hand screen door: the kitchen was dark with a wooden counter and a cement floor, a deep cement basin, many small cupboards and shelves filled with jars of preserved fruit. Unusually for those days, the kitchen led straight into the dining room without any dividing wall or door, there was a long wooden table with many chairs, not all in the same style (Aunt Miems was fashionable long before a magazine could suggest mix-and-match to its readers!), then right, through the door to the lounge. Here my heart beat its wild beat.

Stand with me in the lounge and look towards the small gate for people in jackets. Behind you is the back porch with the kitchen and laundry room on each side. To your left is the door to the dining room, to your right is the door to a bedroom. Around you is lounge furniture, not a set that was delivered in one go, but big, heavy benches and chairs of different kinds of wood, covered in cushions, loose and tight, throws, woven, knitted or crocheted, even tapestries. In front of you is an entrance hall, a wide space with ferns on tall tables and a front door with a top half of coloured glass. No carpet: the front door casts its pattern onto the wooden floor, thank you sun, thank you porch light, there is always this pattern.

From the entrance hall – almost as wide as the lounge – a door on each side, left and right, led to two bedrooms. Thus: a house without a passage! And most importantly: a symmetrical house! If anyone had dared tell me that this wasn't perfect symmetry, I would have argued with him to the end of days. This space was from another time, another world, here my love for – later obsession with – symmetry began. Here I relaxed completely, after this I drew pictures, at home and at school, with absolute symmetry. I still keep searching for such designs, I cannot wear clothes with an asymmetrical design or detail, my stage productions begin and end with symmetry, I wrap gifts with symmetry, lay the table with symmetry, it is my soothing, safe place, small or monumental; when the angels send the rare architect to design a circle, square or rectangle without curls or curves or crooked violence, I am there to exhale, to sigh with pleasure.

I wasn't the only one to receive things there.

There my baby brother was shaped and found his name. It was a Saturday and we were there to braai. The table was laden with Aunt Miems's exuberance, lamb chops, sweet-and-sour onions, creamy potato salad, rice salad with herb confetti, chicken drumsticks with sticky sauce, thick sausages made in this kitchen, chocolate roll with whole cherries and tri-coloured jelly with thick custard.

I was already a plump child with steady and strange habits at the table. For me a braai at this symmetrical temple began with a paper plate heaped with potato salad on the back porch, then a plate of food at the table and then a bowl of pudding back on the porch. Aunt Miems was not the type who believed children should play outside or eat apart, here you could do whatever you wanted, I merely wanted to experience three lovely things at the same time: potato salad, the view (a few steps from the porch there were trees and plants that further on transformed into veld with sharp outgrowths and big rocks and eventually an inaccessible wilderness where secrets lived and infinity started), and finally, the absence of other children (there were one or more boys and my little brother, all at the table!).

On this day, however, my brother was also on his way out and was walking ahead of me. We were gradually discovering that he had a temper that knew no bounds and seldom asked him what he was doing. He pushed open the screen door, followed by me and my small mountain of potato salad. I forgot the door had a spring that always made it slam shut, my brother let go of the door, it hit me like the crack of an oar, I was covered from neck to knees in mayonnaise and flat potatoes.

Mommm! Ian let the door slam!!

Everyone roared with laughter. My brother looked back and laughed until he cried. He was now Ian, my brother.

One evening at dusk, I was in the room, my father was drying the dishes, my mother was drying Ian, the phone rang in the hallway. My father answered. Minutes later, when he thought only my mother was listening, he spoke to her, but I could hear through walls and doors.

Attie got burnt, he said.

On schooldays Uncle Attie drove the school bus, he dropped off the farm children, not everyone wanted to go to boarding school. It was more of a hobby than a job; it was an old bus with a rounded bonnet like in a storybook, he loved the bus like a child, my father and he were constantly on wooden crates, heads in the engine. On this day the bus had broken down on a farm road, there was smoke or steam. Uncle Attie had opened the bonnet and loosened a plug or something and the boiling water had gushed out over him. He was in hospital for months. As a favour my father fixed the bus and twice a day ferried the farm children until Uncle Attie was up and about again.

He and Aunt Miems then invited us over one Sunday afternoon, there were custard biscuits and a fridge tart and sausage rolls and a big present wrapped in light-green patterned paper. Uncle Attie gave a short speech about friendship and support and handed the present to my father. Everyone cried and clapped long enough for me to eat three sausage rolls.

My father opened the present. Inside was a wall clock, not old-fashioned like Grandmother's, also not with curls like The Stoepsusters' cuckoo clock: it was a modern, late-sixties, rectangular brown thing made of a kind of wood that could have been wallpaper. There was a white circle with hands and glass, a little window for the date and another little window through which you could see a swinging silver object. In its darkest heart were a church with a bell and a verger who never slept. Every hour, until the day I wrote matric and left home, it struck; in every lounge of every house to which our family ever moved, it struck. My mother begged, made suggestions, tried to buy new clocks, but my father loved that clock the way Uncle Attie loved his bus, that brown thing travelled with him and sounded the hour until the day he died, every stroke of the clock the recognition he didn't receive elsewhere.

Uncle Attie and Aunt Miems's home has been recreated many times, as paper models, sketches in my diary, several stories in my shows. I have no idea why some things stay with you and others don't, why some things influence you eternally and others do not. I have – as one must – held on to details from centuries-old art-works, characters from classical literature, hidden melodies from studied compositions; inexplicably they keep blowing about like sweet wrappers from an overcrowded train, flutter with rubbish against another man's barbed wire.

Bed, Bible

Being rewarded for something you really do not want to do is probably good, it teaches you discipline and order. That is how circus animals and show horses are rewarded: sweat and you get sugar. At the end of my first school year I got a book prize, I hadn't missed a single day: ring the bell, I report for duty. I was crazy about the ceremony and the book, I still have it. In the front is a certificate and there, in curly black letters, it says: For Attendance. Later I read: You were good for nothing, but you were there.

Ridiculous. It would never happen again. During my second school year I discovered the joys of childhood illnesses. Measles, chickenpox, nausea, headaches, bleeding knee, colds, mumps, I couldn't wait for the next setback. My mother just had to make a diagnosis and write a note for the teacher and, groaning, I could settle in for a holiday – no, a release! – in bed.

So more lifelong and beloved habits were nurtured. To this very day my lounge is a mere passageway, my office nothing more than a storeroom, my porch for guests only, everything that's good, everything that must be, everything memorable, takes place at my table and on or in my bed.

My mother was not at her happiest during my sick days, she already had her hands full with cleaning and Ian who had turned into the most active toddler ever, but she fetched and carried: toast with Marmite, jelly, soup with alphabet noodles, tea with Marie biscuits, cloths for the forehead, Disprins and cough syrup. Why did I have to wait to get ill to live the good life?

Most of the time I was alone in my room. No fever, no cough or ache, just my wonderful bed and me, extra pillows, extra woolly blanket. The headboard had been made by my father, it was in the shape of a cupboard with a long opening for books and stuffed creatures. Here was my Bible, a children's Bible the likes of which I have never seen since. It was a big, fat book with a cover of red imitation leather and golden letters, deeply embossed letters like on a serious historical document. Inside was the entire adult Bible told slightly more simply on snow-white pages, not children's paper, expensive, matte paper like in an encyclopaedia. In between were glossy pages with pictures, not children's pictures with sheep that looked like balls of knitting wool, these were colourful, rich artworks with delicate details, as though painted by famous artists of the Renaissance, each in a very thin black frame. Underneath were captions in small formal letters.

How I loved that Bible! I knew every word and every picture. And the name of every character in every stylised scene. Domes and arches, palm leaves, dark carpets, thrones and tables, silver cups, golden crowns, feather fans, exotic animals, soft drapes from high ceilings, muscled biceps with metal armbands, headdresses with gemstones, swords too magnificent for murder, loaves of bread spilling from baskets, grapes spilling from bowls.

By that time I had already begun to realise that the Whole World consisted of more than just Riebeek-Kasteel, and that was upsetting, but that my friends in the big red Bible could be part of this – such a possibility was simply thrilling; the first shock and disappointment quickly disappeared. Whenever my mother or grandmother or Pretty Derrick (he taught Sunday school even before he got married. Have you ever! said Aunt Gagiano) talked about the Bible, they used words like humility, obedience and gratitude; my treasure chest of imitation leather made me think of things like passion, drama, beauty, suffering and forgiveness. (Did I know these words then? I am sure I did!) They were all there, Mary, Martha, Mary Magdalene, Miriam, Rachel, Ruth, Orpah, Bathsheba, Delilah, Jezebel, Rebecca, Esther, Abraham, Moses, Samuel, David, Jonathan, Samson, Elijah, Peter, Pilate, Herod, Zacchaeus, Lot, Luke, Job, Jonah, Judas, Joseph and Jesus. Each was depicted magnificently, whether he sinned or not, each in a long garment: there were mantles, cords, tassels, braids, beards, chains, fabric that flowed to the ground, nothing was cut or cracked or tangled, folds, texture, light and shadow immortalised their figures in every dream or desire I would ever have. Is it any wonder that for more than thirty years I would begin every performance in a floor-length coat, some kind of regal robe or historical finery?

With or without a fever, there in my bed, absent from all children's activities, an eye and a conviction were formed that would never meet conventional standards; both would be questioned, both would remain unshaken. Could any new idol, preacher, philosopher, sought-after singer or prize-winning writer talk me into a more fashionable viewpoint or a more scientific outlook, tempt me with a more convenient or more intelligent message? They try every day.

To Malmesbury

When are they going to leave us alone? I began wondering this even in Sub B. The whole week you looked forward to Saturday, no school, no getting up early, no ugly clothes, no yelling, only your own plans. But every Saturday the devil was among us: sport nonsense, markets, bazaars, fêtes, weddings, street braais, funerals, horse riding, farm visits, birthday parties, more and more, again and again, they couldn't stop, they thought things up, carted tables around, parked in the dust, set out chairs, turned on gas stoves, took baskets from car boots, arranged cups and saucers, carved biltong, danced in circles, sang in the round, prayed in groups, cried in each other's arms, there was no end!

The house angel must have heard my silent screams, because gradually empty Saturdays began to appear, just one a month, but I was relieved and thankful. On these blissful days we could get in the car and go to Malmesbury. I was no longer confused or furious about all the towns that had appeared in the Whole World. We could get away.

In the centre of Malmesbury was a surprisingly big store, a handsome building with different levels; here you could buy anything. There were counters that identified the different departments, here girls in neat blouses set out boxes and drawers in front of you, you could touch and choose. Afterwards you put your cash on the counter. A girl folded up your money and slip and put it in a peculiar metal cocoon above her head. She pulled a chain and the cocoon shot away and sailed along a cable to a central glass office high in the sky. A network of cables was strung above our heads like a web, cocoons shot this way and that. Ian was beside himself with happiness – he was four years old and discovering technical inventions.

Buy more! he yelled when our cocoon came back with change.

We're going to Die Teepot now, my mother said.

Immediately, Ian was furious.

Buy more! he yelled again.

Look at that! my father said quickly.

Two cable cocoons zipped past us, Ian bellowed with joy. A few minutes later we were sitting in front of Die Teepot in the car, Father had gone inside to get hamburgers. Long before chain restaurants got rid of natural smells and flavours, Die Teepot in Malmesbury's high street prepared take-away meals. Every free Saturday we picked up hamburgers and ate them under the trees just outside town. Father parked in the shade, the windows were rolled down and Mother searched until soft jazz played on the radio. We each opened up the crisp white paper and studied our hamburger. Unlike all others known to man, Die Teepot's burgers contained no lettuce, sliced tomato or cheese. A flat homemade meatball was covered in caramelised onion, that was all. And it was every feast I could think off, folded up in a fresh bun.

Ian's temper immediately flared. He began scraping off the onion with his finger, ending up, like every other time, with a hamburger in one hand and a paper full of onion in the other.

My paper is finished, he growled.

My father's shoulders began shaking, he knew if Ian saw him laughing all hell would break loose, but he couldn't help himself. My mother immediately grabbed the handful of onion, my father quickly passed him his wrapper. By the time the growing storm had been driven off, my hamburger was finished. Before the Americans had decided an early death was essential, a hamburger was very small, and there weren't any chips. I was so hungry I could eat a seat. On cooler days there were containers of ice cream you ate with a wooden spoon, a paltry consolation. The one time my father bought ice cream on a hot day, Ian's melted and a frightening explosion followed.

These Malmesbury times were a respite. I remember the jazz – in those days local music was at a particularly low point, and without commenting my mother would turn the radio's knob until she heard something stylish, Frank Sinatra, Bing Crosby, Lena Horne or Tony Bennett. I sat in the back of the car and listened, looked at the rows of magical tree trunks and wondered who (WHO??) was full after one hamburger.

The First Soldier

When you can choose how a story begins, it goes without saying that the first sound will be the pounding of horses' hooves. An unpaved road – one that doesn't give off dust or mud or lets loose pebbles shoot into the air – winds through a dark-green forest, six white horses with white plumes effortlessly pull a black coach decorated with swirls and curls in old gold. Young guards bounce elegantly on pitch-black horses, in another era they would have earned fame as models and pop stars, now all of them are dressed in spotless white tights, long shining boots, short embroidered jackets and white gloves. Their swords rest in engraved scabbards with brightly coloured jewels. Possibly there is a princess in the coach, perhaps the difficult mother of a nobleman, perhaps an unwilling groom on his way to a forced wedding, but the revelation never takes place; all the attention now shifts to the castle on the horizon. The woods on both sides of the road have disappeared, light-green vineyards are now visible, a silver river flows underneath a bridge with statues of half-dressed heroes from classical literature, rows of manservants stream out of the castle and form a line on either side of the entrance.

Now the unpaved road should turn into a surface of smooth, intricately patterned stone, but instead it becomes rougher, a sharp pebble digs into my foot. I stand still and lift my foot, there is no blood. I look behind me, there is no forest or river, only our home. I look ahead again. The castle and manservants have disappeared.

Opposite our house a short, untarred street began and then ended on the edge of town. This was known as The One Side Street. Here visitors only looked ahead or to the one side, left on the way there, right on the way back. There were three erfs on the one side (so, to my left at this moment): the first was empty, just unmown grass (and snakes! The Stoepsusters warned), then the tall house with the double garage, here lived my friend and her divorced mother, a cruel woman who never let us play inside, then a house with a man and a woman who walked with difficulty and didn't like children, then a narrow side street, then a house with a small orchard, then a corner house and then the last street. On the other side of The One Side Street, to my right, were The Earth Houses, a row of stuffy little houses, small and low to the ground. On the street side were limp fences, dilapidated chicken wire sagging from crooked posts and covered with granadillas and other creepers. It looked like these fences were pulling the little houses into the ground. And some people believed that was what was happening. Perhaps the inhabitants as well, they were all elderly and suspicious, scrubbing with a pail or a basin in the hand, none of them capable of smiling, not even a slight nod.

The day those houses are gone, we'll plant trees, fruit trees, so we can make jam! Aunt Gagiano said.

At the last street I turn left and walk to the long house without a front garden. Past the front door and the narrow veranda, directly on the street, is a tall wooden gate painted brown that forms an arch at the top. It is a double gate that pushes open like the stable doors of a manor house, but here it takes you to an untidy garden with loquat trees, house on the left, garage on the right.

The Le Rouxs: not family of ours, just good friends of my parents; up until the woman's death more than forty years later she and my mother were bosom friends. There were two sons, if there were more then I, as with my little brother at that stage, was unaware of their presence. The younger son was my age and the elder was a grown-up, perhaps in high school, perhaps at college, perhaps working. Grown-up.

At the time the horse-drawn coach began appearing and disappearing, most of my perceptions were still without name or category, and although I was too young to put it into words or understand it fully (after years of literature, movies, paintings and conviction it still wasn't me but a friend who first said the words 'Born at the wrong time, in the wrong place' out loud), I was already dead sure that I was completely alone in my survival or mission in this place, whether town or planet.

Alone I push the brown stable door open. I walk in, the door to the garage on my right is open. I peek inside. It smells of cement and the oil my grandfather always rubs into his woodwork. There is no car, no window, it's a workshop, two bulbs hang from a beam. The elder Le Roux boy stands next to a high countertop. A piece of wood is turning in circles and the machine purrs like a happy cat. He leans over and pushes an object against the piece of wood.

I haven't learnt yet about fixation or taboo or lust or love, but I know he is more beautiful than anything in our town. He has an unreal shape, muscled and tanned, and must therefore be one of the grown-up men who look away or keep busy when I arrive. But he doesn't look away, he shuts down the machine and smiles broadly.

Come in, he says, My mother isn't here right now. Or did you come to visit me?

I turn around to see who he is talking to.

Have you seen a lathe before? he asks, Come see, you clamp the wood like this and as soon as it starts turning, you can make anything with the chisel. I'm making new feet for my mother's old table, her jelly jiggles when we have dinner.

He laughs with an open mouth and rows of snow-white teeth.

My mother makes a lot of jelly, I say.

I'd been ready to pick loquats or perhaps get a rusk from the lady; in no way was I prepared for a conversation with a friendly giant. I hate my face and my rubber body and my crooked little teeth, I know I have seven childish freckles, two on each cheek, three on my nose, I can feel how each of them jumps off me and flies into everything in the workshop like dazed bees. How can I escape? Will I turn around and try to run like lead? Will I keep blushing until I explode?

My mother says you draw really well, he says. You should bring your things, then you can come and draw here. I work here every afternoon, one day my father is going to chase me away and say I must go work or learn, but I like making pretty things.

I stand and wait for my freckles to land again.

Okay, I say, I'll bring my things.

Outside I struggle, it is much more difficult to pull the stable gate shut than to push it open. I never saw him again. I walked back home along the untarred road. There was no announcement, the air didn't change colour, but I walked a different, a completely new road to the one I had been walking only a few minutes earlier. In those moments I had been changed. Within months we would move to a new town, I would arrive there as a new child, to all appearances the same, a scared, cautious creature with a soft face and big eyes filled with worry, ready to duck or to run, but on the inside was a newborn courage that I myself wouldn't recognise at first; sleeping it lay, waiting to push me forward the next time I wanted to run away or turn back too easily.

The changed me walked back along The One Side Street. I had met my first soldier. Until a few moments ago I had run in circles on a straight road, like a young fool with his even more foolish underlings, Upset and Doubt; now I walked, though still freckled, with a straight back. I felt light and safe, unaware that The First Soldier would multiply into a whole battalion of fighters. I cannot deny or disguise this truth, unbelievably and inexplicably this is my reality: ever since I closed the stable gate for the last time, throughout the rest of my life, in school, at university, working, adult, established, sick, healthy, exalted or exposed, always unexpectedly, but as if according to a timetable, strong, heterosexual, professional, resourceful men appear in my life, men who function comfortably and often within the norm, each with an instinct to protect me, to support me and defend me with passion, without duty or agenda. I get to know their wives, spend time with their children, pour wine when there are questions or stories. Those who notice this are still astonished; I am surrounded by characters who should by all the usual rules of logic have dismissed me.

There are few miracles and no guarantees. I will always dream of coaches, linger near candlelight, stumble under insults, glare jealously at the comfort ignorance brings. But every now and then, when darkness grows heavy, when only sleep can soothe, I know I can fall, far and without check; it is a luxury you only receive with the knowledge that soldiers, each within reach, are always ready to draw a sword from a scabbard, without hesitation.

On the way back home I knew nothing of this. But how I would need that help in the decade until and including matric, throughout those ten years when my country's leaders, its preachers, its parents and pedagogues would experience an obtuse, chauvinistic, racist, sexist, homophobic, self-righteous, petty, super-stupid panic that would smother every blossoming young soul until belief, music, art and knowledge lay gasping beneath condemnation and ugly clothes. It was known as the seventies.

The Game is Heavy

I am standing in front of Grandmother's dressing table. The top
drawer is open. If you didn't know her and only saw the drawer,
you would picture a completely different person. The drawer is
full of necklaces, too formal a word, instead we spoke of beads.
All are in the same style, each a different colour, two or three
strings, short, slightly longer, a bit longer still, all ending in the
same clasp or stone that lies at the nape of the neck. From back
to front the beads get bigger. Not one is completely round, each
looks like it has been pressed with a finger into a unique shape.
What they're made of I don't know. In the corner of the drawer is
a broken string with splinters like thin glass or shell. Each bead
has been dipped in another colour paint or enamel, no colour is
solid, there are variations like when you mix two paint colours
and decorate something with rough brushstrokes. These strings
look exactly like those the Queen of England wears in photos,
only more colourful: Grandmother's rainbow pearls. They lie like
half-moons in the drawer – one dark blue, one soft pink, one light
green, one blood red, one mustard yellow, one turquoise – and
welcome me to a new heaven.

Grandmother, I say, In my Bible all the kings wear beads like these.

Grandmother laughs.

Then try the red one, she says.

I put the string of beads around my neck, Grandmother fastens it at the back.

They wear long mantles, I say.

Then we'll have to see what we've got, Grandmother says.

She takes an orange-red dress from the wardrobe, soft and with patterns like flames, inside is a lining in dull red, I have never seen her in this gown. I don't ask questions, I just hold my breath while she lets the fire column fall in folds around my body. She digs in a shopping bag and a long-deceased animal lands on my shoulders. Hare? Jackal? I have never seen Grandmother wear fur. Now I look like the Queen of England's mother.

Do your kings have crowns? asks Grandmother.

Yes, Grandmother, I say, Golden ones!

Let's go look in the front room, she says.

I lift the front of the dress and look at my feet.

Those kings wore sandals, says Grandmother, We don't have things like that.

She bends down in front of the wardrobe and turns around with two black court shoes in her hands.

Don't fall, she says.

I shuffle behind her into the front room. The shoes have heels, it is a revelation, a steadfast fortress, an elevation above the rest of humanity, what wretched creature decided we had to tackle any kind of life in flat shoes?

In the corner of the front room lives a smallish fern on a wooden stand. Around the clay pot is a metal cylinder with curls and spikes that point upward, painted a dull gold. Grandmother lifts the fern in its pot, slips off the cylinder and carefully places it on my head.

Down the hallway, she says, Your subjects await you!

By the time I reach the end of the hallway, I am no longer a king, I am myself and Grandmother is the mercy without which no nine-year-old could ever have a future.

* * *

We were in Wellington's cemetery for an hour: Grandmother went to take flowers, sweet peas, nasturtiums, arum lilies and purple flowers that look like paper. I don't know whose graves she chose, death was not yet a reality to me. Aunt Engela Hamman was there too, she fetched buckets of water from the tap. I ran from angel to angel. This was before Wellington's vandalism started and the cemetery was still a place of beauty.

Now I'm sitting in the back of Aunt Hamman's big car full of shiny-shiny handles, Grandmother is sitting in the passenger seat in front, we drive past the Andrew Murray church, we don't turn right to where the main road's big shops wait, we drive straight on down the road to the station, here the shops are still one-one and this is where Grandmother prefers to do her shopping.

Aunt Hamman is dressed in soft brown trousers with stitching from top to bottom, a thin brown jersey with a round neck, a second thin brown jersey that hangs from her shoulders and two long gold chains with small rust-brown stones finger-lengths from one another. (No, these aren't tiger's eyes, she says.) Her hair is dark with light-grey streaks, sprayed into obedient waves. She was grand on weekdays as well.

Grandmother is in one of her tailored dresses, this one a favourite in coral pink. She is wearing stockings, dark court shoes with low heels and, apart from her delicate watch, no jewellery. Her unique strings of beads were only for births, weddings and deaths. Grandmother was known to everyone. Anyone could tell you about her smile, round cheeks and laughing eyes. The picture was completed by her short, curly dark hair (I cannot remember a grey hair or find one in a photo), no make-up and an alert, erect posture.

Grandmother's clothes were never discussed, she never wondered aloud like other women what she should wear to this place or that place. She lived close to the ground, was every waking moment serving or consoling or helping; chatter about nonsense like clothes was unthinkable. Still, she did something I would only observe years later among the famous or eccentrics with unlimited funds and permanent homes in the media: she wore a uniform, fitted to the millimetre. She wasn't a thin woman, yet much too active to be big; the kitchen was her headquarters and her curves corroborated her love of food, her perfect calves testified to an extraordinary energy.

She wore dresses perfectly fitted to her body, always with a boat neck, always with sleeves to just past the elbow, each with a small slit for movement, each dress ending just below the knees, tighter towards the bottom, a small slit at the back. Did someone make them for her? Was there a shop that only sold these dresses? When would Grandmother linger before a shelf to pick out a piece of cloth? The fabrics were expensive, wrinkle-free and always plain, no patterns. There were a few grander versions, these were made of a smoother fabric, almost too stiff to fold nicely, each with a short jacket of the same fabric, one with a coat. These creations had designs with dramatic flowers or other strong motifs, all in brushstrokes like the texture of her beads.

Too late I began to wonder about this. Too late to ask questions. How incredibly modern! How intelligent! How elegant! How practical! How flattering! My grandmother, who only used a magazine to put herself to sleep, was far ahead of her con temporaries in matters of style. As a grown man I am obsessed with clothes, I buy pieces from around the world, work with designers, comb through each new collection, and it all con tributes to one daily outfit: black stretch pants, black shirt with zip, black tailored jacket, black pointy shoes. Uniform. Grandmother.

Here and there we stop in front of shops. A few parcels appear next to me on the seat. Mince in brown paper. Butter in waxed paper. Lamb chops in white paper. Sardines in newspaper.

Are we done? asks Aunt Hamman.

Yes, thank you, says Grandmother, Let's get back to the house, I can already taste the tea.

I look at the parcels.

Is this all? I ask.

Grandmother and Aunt Hamman laugh.

We are poor in cents but rich in people, says Grandmother.

That's nature, says Aunt Hamman, And he comes to those who honour him, people are only messengers.

I understand what she is saying. People turned up almost daily with baskets full of tangerines (the vegetable garden fence was often festooned with hundreds of strips of dried peel, Grandmother's secret in many dishes), basins of harders, bags of loquats, bowls of mulberries, buckets of grapes, crates of peaches. Grandmother bottled, stored, served, shared.

In the late afternoon, Grandfather comes into the kitchen. He looks at the worktop. He looks at the stove. He looks at the oven. He looks at the table. He looks at Grandmother.

Are you expecting the Israelites again? he asks.

Ben, do you still not know your own home? laughs Aunt Hamman.

In the evening we sit at the table, the one in the kitchen. As always, many have arrived. A small woman with half a pair of sunglasses, she lost one eye because of a poisonous bug, the woman who doesn't want to believe her parakeet is gone, the man who works on the college grounds, the minister whose wife doesn't talk or cook, the girl whose sister landed in the machine at the jam factory and later was buried as 600 tins (that morning Grandmother was at her grave as well), and a friend's son who drives all the way from Paarl every time Grandmother announces that she's making meatballs.

Grandmother makes chunky meatballs with big pieces of caramelised onion, sultanas and torn bits of bread: she believes smooth, evenly sized meatballs give you nightmares, they make you dream of cricket or bowls. Apart from the meatballs we eat yellow rice with lots of parsley, sweet pumpkin, green beans and baby potatoes, all from the garden. Also buttermilk pudding served with berries from the garden. We eat gloriously, too much and organic.

I know I'm sitting in front of a pudding, but what do I smell? says Aunt Hamman. She sniffs the air.

The sweet potatoes! yells Grandmother, I forgot!

She yanks open the warming drawer, a casserole of steaming sweet potatoes appears on the table.

Butter! Sugar! Cinnamon! says Grandmother and scurries to the cupboard.

Aren't we full yet? asks Aunt Hamman.

Not at all, says Grandmother, Tomorrow it's war, today we eat! Whoo, the game is heavy!

I always thought that was something everybody said, but later learnt it was only Grandmother's saying. She said this when she was at her happiest, surrounded by people, and in the conviction that things could not be better.

* * *

We are sitting on the long back porch. We are lounging like three lobsters in boiling water; it's hot all over. Grandmother has a wet cloth on the back of her neck, Grandfather has one on his chest, I have one on my forehead.

Are the car's windows open? asks Grandmother.

Yes, says Grandfather.

Is the car under cover? asks Grandmother.

Yes, says Grandfather.

Then it's not so hot that you can't drive, says Grandmother.

Drive? says Grandfather, Now?

The child has been visiting for five days and he hasn't had an ice cream yet, says Grandmother, Or when do you think it will be hot enough?

Where should we go? asks Grandfather.

There's ice cream at the swimming pool, says Grandmother. You don't have to pay to swim, you buy it at the little window. It's two minutes from here. And don't buy that soft white stuff that comes out of the machine, it melts before it's even in the cone. Buy him rum and raisin, they serve it in a bowl, it's ice cold and lasts longer.

Grandfather and I get into the Beetle equally unwillingly. I know he's not in the mood for me, he prefers his grandchildren in a group, then he can tell his stories with the required effect and doesn't have to look anyone in the eye. I am filled with fear (I never knew you could be scared in such heat) – the town's swimming pool has everything I detest: yelling children, water and music over loudspeakers. Like every other time I get anxious, I talk the whole two-minute drive without stopping to catch my breath. We park at the swimming pool. I smell chlorine and suntan lotion even before we get to the little window. Hell of the hell's hell.

Grandfather asks for cigarettes and a bowl of rum and raisin. We get back into the Beetle. Relief. Grandfather drives around the corner. He stops underneath a big tree in front of a small building with three shop doors.

Wait here, he says and gets out.

He goes in at the furthest door. Bottle store, I read. I eat my ice cream. Grandfather opens the door and puts a paper bag with three bottles of wine on the back seat. In our family wine never appears at the table. No one sits with wine on the porch. No one talks about wine. I lick my spoon and keep dead quiet. Back at the house I get out and run to the porch. Grandmother sits with a fresh wet cloth draped over her face. Grandfather slips into the garden shed with the wine.

And how was it? asks Grandmother.

Nice, thank you, Grandmother, I say.

Where's your grandfather? she asks.

In the garden shed, I say.

We sit for twenty minutes. Then we smell the cigarette, Grandfather is smoking by the vegetable garden's fence.

I think it's time we start making the ginger beer, says Grandmother, Come and help me.

In the kitchen she takes the bottle opener from the drawer. We are out the door again, across the porch, down the steps, across the back yard to the garden shed. At the pile of potatoes Grandmother bends down and rolls away the top ones. One by one the three bottles of wine appear. One has been drunk from and the cork has been pushed back in. Grandmother pulls all three corks and upends the bottles.

It smells like school pee, I say.

It tastes like that too, says Grandmother.

We walk back to the kitchen. Grandmother rinses the bottles and stands them upside down on the drying rack. She holds five fingers in the air.

Sugar, yeast, ginger, lemon, raisins, she says and opens the cupboard.

* * *

Grandfather was a storyteller. At every gathering the grandchildren sat in a half-moon at his feet and he filled us with wonder and especially terror. He often started like this: One day, far down the road, a puff of dust appears. And it's coming closer and closer. What could it be?

A daldoel! all of us would yell.

A daldoel was a hairy monster, upright like a human, slightly shorter than a grown man, wild, vicious and unpredictable enough to eat a small child. That was the only description he gave us, the rest was left to our young imaginations, we could adjust and adapt the details as the adventures took place. Grandfather's own imagination was boundless, barbaric and fantastic in the extreme. He made up words and changed names, nothing was ordinary, Paarl was called the Cape of Johannesburg, the river was Other Mister's River, a fishcake was Goliath's Dead Eye.

Grandfather also drew comic strips in and on the back of Grandmother's letters. Gross and engrossing, each a work of art. When you looked at them you could hear Grandmother clicking her tongue. With thin, shaky lines he sketched the way she spent her days. A personal favourite (I still often look at it) was the one showing Grandmother pulling a big mole from a gutter. Underneath he wrote: Grandmother catches dinner.

Grandmother was a letter writer. Once or twice a month we received a letter, addressed to the whole family; without exception each of us was also addressed separately somewhere. First we read the envelope. On the front: Mister Postman, thank you for delivering my news so regularly to my children. On the back: I've already sealed it but cannot find a stamp. I don't know why a thing doesn't stay where you've put it. Oh, it's starting to rain, I'm going to make pancakes. I know the batter should rest first, but it's already four o'clock. Kisses. The letter itself started above the date or the salutation with a late inscription: Yesterday Daleen called, she says Hennie's back is acting up again.

Letters were written on thin white or light-blue paper. Writing paper with patterns, flowers, stars or just coloured designs in the corners was high fashion, but Grandmother preferred an empty page; she wrote until even the smallest space was filled. One day she gave me a writing pad with circles of many-coloured dots around each page. That was during the time when my handicraft monster first reared its head, my love of rows began to flower and my dedication to repetition began in earnest.

With writing pad, scissors and sellotape I sit in the front room and lose all track of time, I cut and glue lanterns, I learnt to do this in art class, but then there was only one; now I make a hundred. With each finished lantern my life becomes more beautiful. For the first time ever I miss lunch, I don't realise that Grandmother has left the house and have no idea where Grandfather is.

I go and look for the man who works on the college grounds. He ties a wire to one end of the long porch, right underneath the eaves. We string lanterns along the wire until it is full, he ties it to the other end of the porch. Immediately the porch is unrecognisable. We do it again, twice. Eventually we stand under a cloud of lanterns. I cannot believe what I have made. Who has a camera?

A car stops outside, Grandmother and her church friend appear on the porch, each with two big bags.

Oh, that's pretty, says Grandmother, My grandchild is bursting with talent!

My arms! says the church friend.

They storm into the kitchen, I am right behind them. They put the bags on the table and begin to unpack. Light-blue boxes. Ten, twelve, eighteen, twenty-five, thirty-eight, fifty!

What is it? I ask.

Budgie seed, says Grandmother, Isn't it sweet?

And who has a budgie? asks Grandfather at the back door.

It was on promotion, says Grandmother, It was so cheap! I couldn't just leave it there!

What are you going to do with it? asks Grandfather.

If a budgie turns up here one day, we'll be ready! says Grandmother.

Well, you'll have to clear the table, says Grandfather, The woman with the kumquats is on her way over, tomorrow morning at five you'll have to start pricking.

What is pricking? I ask.

We call it pricking, says Grandmother, But we make a very small cross at one end of each kumquat. Then we start to rinse them. We quickly boil them three times in fresh water. A kumquat is a jewel of a thing, but as bitter as your cousins' other grandmother. Only once the bitter is gone you start boiling it with sugar. Tonight it's early dinner and early to bed.

The next morning, the sun is still weak, I walk into the kitchen. Pots and pots of kumquats fill the room. Grandmother sits on a chair, her head rests on the table, she snores gently.

Grandmother? I ask.

She lifts her head.

Who is here? What did I miss? she asks.

I say, Grandmother was sleeping.

She looks at me.

I was waiting for the sun, she says, I finished with the last rinse ages ago, it was still dark. Your grandfather is a rubbish, he does it every time I get fruit, wakes me at midnight and says it's five o'clock.

What now? I ask.

I have to wait for yesterday's church lady, then we start to boil them, says Grandmother, She's small enough to stand on the chair, then she stirs with the long stick. But we're awake now, I'll make breakfast.

We sit at either side of the table. We eat yoghurt that Grandmother makes with the starter. It is slightly sour with small pieces of peach, better than any swimming-pool ice cream. Afterwards we eat homemade white bread, the big square one with the hard crust. On each thick slice Grandmother spreads salted butter, on top comes roughly grated golden-yellow Wellington cheese.

If only all people could taste this, they would stop looking for trouble, says Grandmother.

She gets up and lifts the tall pot from the stove. She pours coffee into two cups.

It's just for smelling and dunking, she says, If you drink this neat your stomach will growl for days.

Then she takes rusks from the tin with the light-green stripes, four long pieces full of aniseed.

Whoo, the game is heavy, she says.

The game is heavy, I say.

Samuel

It must be terrible to have an ordinary grandfather or grand-mother. I have had contact with real, living beings who described grandparents with words like strict, shy, sour, frazzled, frail, cynical, sceptical, superstitious, scared, angry or absent. My grandfather and grandmother (I only knew one pair, my father's parents had died before I was born) were on any given day – good or difficult – a tour de force, a knockout blow, a team of trek oxen, a fit of laughter, a film, a circus, an army, a fort, a season.

Grandmother was unpredictable, energetic, hospitable and unique, exactly how I would like to be remembered. Grandfather was unpredictable, funny, full of stories and often moody, exactly how I am remembered.

Everybody, everybody knew my grandmother. In the family she was Grandmother Maria, in town she was Aunt Ben. Why even the most imposing women were saddled with their husbands' names for generations will never be clear to me, but Uncle and Aunt Ben were beloved and treated this title as a tribute.

It must be terrible to have a grandfather or grandmother with an ordinary home. Grandchildren – and there were more than ten of us – must be bewitched and beguiled for at least six of their first eight years, walk with their feet in the air, see the impossible when awake and dream the improbable when asleep. They must know that attics and staircases are home to roof trolls and spy moths, that groaning beams mean that the cavaliers and the cadavers are breaking their chains, that when motes of dust begin to dance in a beam of light, elves and talking butterflies aren't far behind, that paths can walk and destinations can wander to prevent anyone from ever losing their way.

Grandfather and Grandmother lived in a castle, one with an infinite number of rooms, a bell tower, a ballroom with a grand piano, a hallway that went on longer than a sermon, with the highest ceilings a child could ever see, porches on three sides and two trees that could see everything. Big Tree One was a rubber tree with roots too big for the earth, these roots lived above ground, grey and smooth like the feet of a prehistoric beast; a bit further away was Big Tree Two (an oak?) with a trunk so thick ten human arms were needed for an embrace, and at the top, a green cloud in which a house could hide.

For the uninformed and distant acquaintances, this situation was too overwhelming, so their truth went like this: Grandfather was the factotum at the Hugenote Kollege in Wellington. Here girls were trained in social work. There were two campuses, on one of these there were two residences, three houses and a smallish hall. One of these residences was a colossal white building with many windows, a small tower and a big front door. Part of the ground floor had been set up as Grandfather and Grandmother's home – their front porch was a side porch, their front door was a side door. This building was known as House Samuel. To us, the castle's regular guests, it was a living sphere, the stage set on which a masterwork was enacted over many years, still known as Samuel.

Samuel's nerve centre was the kitchen, bigger than a restaurant's. And with a cold room! Could I ever forget the heavy steel door with the massive chrome handle?! On holidays this was where the family gathered and Grandmother bustled, as though an industrial kitchen was the norm for any housewife.

Grandmother, why can you walk into the fridge?

Like the wolf would say, all the better to eat, my child. Now the girls are eating over at Gesie, but in the past all their meals were prepared here. I'm not being mean, but they can eat a lot, those plain girls. When you choose a life of caring and serving, there's little pleasure to be had.

What is serving, Grandmother?

You worry about others. And nobody pays you lots of money to do it. A big inheritance or a rich husband is your only hope, but that doesn't happen often. Poor things, I often leave out rusks and rolls in front by the piano, it's not my job, I bake for you – take another biscuit – but they don't have a mother close by.

In front by the piano. Here I first chilled the family's blood with a full-scale performance. At the end of Grandmother's hallway there was a door that was pushed open during college vacations.

It led to the long passage with Samuel's official front door at the end, and next to it the big room. Here there was a brown grand piano, as out of tune as all school pianos, but a magnet with an attraction *just* greater than my appetite. Every Christmas, while banquets were being prepared, while my mother laughed with her sisters and sisters-in-law on the porch, while uncles passed the time like only uncles could, while Grandfather hid in the garden shed, while cousins slid down Samuel's stairs on mattresses, I planned the Christmas concerts at the grand piano.

First Grandmother's hundreds of Christmas cards were brought in and displayed. Paper chains were made and strung where a child could reach. Pine boughs were dragged in. Candles were planted in any container that could glitter, and then the casting was done. Costumes appeared from Grandmother's wardrobe, supplemented by bed linen, pelts, creepers and cloth flowers. Unwilling children were immediately replaced by myself – with the exception of the shepherds and their sheep I wanted to play every character. (Shepherds and sheep were interchangeable, draped in bathmats and seat covers from the college's bakkie.) Only much later, after I'd started reading in earnest, did I realise how far-reaching my designs had been: over the years Mary had appeared as Mata Hari, the ghostly woman from Wilkie Collins's famous novel, and also Isadora Duncan. Joseph and his fleece looked like the leader of a Viking tribe and the angel was more a lady of the night. Only when enough jewellery was left over did a wise man or two appear. One year there were also appearances by Herod, Potiphar and Cleopatra. I remember the last concert in Samuel as a particular highlight: it was the world's first nativity scene with a mermaid.

Isn't anybody going to put a stop to it? my mother asked every year.

Let him be, Grandmother said, Have you ever seen a happier child?

It was too late to turn back, a monster was born. Everyone had to attend the performances. And they had to pay. And sit still. Applause, no talking. Only Grandfather wasn't there. The first year, he saw me try on a headdress one afternoon and had to go and have a cigarette on the porch. Until his dying day he never once saw me perform. There was never a rude word or a surprised look or a question, he just went out to the porch or the shed.

The one who did suffer was my mother's eldest brother, he simply couldn't look at me, not during the Christmas concert or in the hallway or in the garden or at the table or when we said goodbye. He was gentle and friendly, but he couldn't look. After the Samuel years I saw him once more at a funeral and stayed out of his way, we never spoke a word. My other two uncles endured and adapted; my mother's youngest brother – heavens, but he was handsome! – even made jokes and often laughed at the increasingly odd things I would say.

The women sat in a row and watched as year after year I tried to convince my audience that Mary did, in fact, wear strings of fake pearls, as did the rest of Bethlehem's residents. They laughed, sang along, prayed quietly and wondered in whispers how my parents would ever tame this spectacle.

Cousins followed their instincts as cousins do, a few did their own thing, a few immediately agreed when I proposed yet another ambitious project (adult baptism in the river was a perennial favourite), even made suggestions or insisted on shared leadership. I grew to love them and together we still long for Samuel.

The river: did the water follow them or did they follow the water? Grandfather and Grandmother were always near a river. Samuel's river came at the end of the Five Phases of Euphoria. You couldn't just take a car or walk around a corner, for these phases you had to leave by Grandmother's front door (Samuel's side door). Here the building was shaped like a U: there was a big, high porch with a roof and hard benches, in the middle of the porch was a small lawn, in the corner of the lawn was a tree, Euphoria One, a tree unlike any other in our story. Its trunk was narrow and twisted gracefully before branching into an open hand with long fingers. Leaves were silver green and smooth as plastic, in between were the flowers, red-pink, firmly shaped like lilies born from small pomegranates. The smell was the smell of Grandmother's house, these flowers were everywhere, in glasses, in shallow bowls, in saucers, next to beds, on windowsills, on a tray in the front room. This tree (with Magdel's help I recently discovered it's called a camellia) looked like an emblem of the East and I called every footstep from the front door by name: step, step, step, step, Japan, Japan, Japan, stair, stair, stair, Euphoria Two.

Euphoria Two, a big gravelled piece of ground, was ruled by Big Trees One and Two; they allowed us to park, to play for hours or to stare at the Endless Green. The last three Phases of Euphoria consisted of field upon field of green, each different; I thought of it as a desert that had been rescued. (This was what I prayed for right through each of the dry, deadly holidays we had to survive when my mother's one sister still lived in South-West and it was believed that screaming children on a sand dune was an expression of joy.)

After the gravel there was a slope where Big Tree One's massive roots tumbled like an Inca temple cut from a sacred rock, here we could sidestep down to a lawn, also a stream and carpets of nasturtiums and arum lilies. Here a vineyard began, stretching as far to the left and as far to the right as the eye could see, light green and lush and without a single grape. It was a vineyard for walking through, planted only for your eyes. A narrow path with long, flattened grass led to the last Euphoria, Donkiebos, a destination more seductive than the biggest toy store. Each terror and flight and retreat of my life has been the result of association, but even after a nameless uncle by marriage had a stroke here and was carried by my father and others along the vineyard path back to Samuel, all this green never lost its charm.

Donkiebos began with a neat row of trees, a border that didn't want to keep anything out, a neat paper wood from a pop-up book, with everything that belonged in a friendly wood on the inside, the sound of hundreds of radio birds (the same ones that in the days of radio dramas had to signal any outside scene), a ceiling of green that only here and there allowed the sun to draw patterns, a knee-high cosmos of saplings that rose hopefully in the shadows of their elders and a thick carpet of seasons' worth of fallen leaves, soft and in the many shades of mortality. Here I decided that no rake would ever despoil a home of mine, that no suburban garden would ever announce my presence. Nowadays, in a small forest that has taken me more than twenty years to establish and ecstatically let flourish, bewildered guests often gasp: No garden service? You're just leaving it? What on earth! (Yes! Earth!)

Partway into Donkiebos you could hear the river – stream, rather. There are words I've never wanted to use again after primary school, burble is one, but this little river burbled, lightly lapped, kissed stones, danced around bowed branches like a wet ballerina, everything that was lovely and sweet and good flowed in front of you. It was the picture to which every pharmacy almanac, get-well-soon card, spiritual diary and amateur watercolourist still aspires. Here I should state clearly: apart from rain, I – for reasons known and unknown – have no interest whatsoever in water. Shallow water and tame waves are only entered under duress, oceans, waterfalls, outside showers, swimming pools and fishponds are made for others. Even as a young child I fiercely protected my triangle of trees, books and snacks, why bother me because other children have to paddle and pee everywhere there's water?

BUT. The stream in Donkiebos kept calling to me. In the early years we went there in groups, later only Grandmother and I went (once the two of us decided that she would petition the government to ban rakes) and eventually just me on my own. It is still difficult to explain what started here.

Running water reflects light, a clear stream whose bed is visible even more so. There are sunbeams, dragonflies, bees, bugs, fish, small creatures with eyes, the radio birds, broken glass or other sins, many things that will make you believe you are seeing something else. But I did – when it was quiet and I felt safe enough to forget about myself or the constant possibility of another for a moment – begin to see outlines, call it sketches above the water, dim flashes, things that moved, for a second or less, an un-known thing that could fly without a whole body, later still, sus-pended creatures, transparent, that began to take shape, always from bottom to top, and then disappeared before arms or a face appeared, once the hem of a garment that touched the water and then was lifted away. Nothing was visible enough that I could talk of it out loud or convince someone of anything real. Children would say, Oh, you're crazy! Grown-ups would say: Too much sun! Too much sugar! You are tired, your eye is twitching!

So, I kept quiet. But I would see. Soon. The figures would appear without tricks, without doubt, clearly. And nearby. Only a few hundred metres away.

Shutters with Moon

It is a square room, pure white and small. The first door to the right when you come through Grandmother's Samuel front door. It is my bedroom when I come to visit, on my own or with the family or with the whole clan, it's my room.

I lie in bed, the light is off, but I can see everything, Grandmother has left the window and the shutters open, it's a warm night. The bed is next to the wall, at its foot there is a wardrobe, a tall, narrow wardrobe of dark wood, not cheap plywood like the typical sixties furniture, but still thin, a simple, light wardrobe. No feet, an arch has been cut at the bottom of each of the four sides. Grandmother says it's for reaching the dust, you have to be able to clean under a cupboard, it keeps your soul bright and your steps light.

Next to the wardrobe is the door, higher than doors in other houses and painted white. The door ends in the corner. This is the width of the room: wardrobe and door. Then an empty wall that runs parallel to the bed up to the window. The window is next to the head of the bed. One side wardrobe and door, the other side head and window. This is the whole room.

Before, there had been a small painting on the big wall, a water-colour of a house and a yard in a wooden frame without embellishment. One day the painting had disappeared and a great-grandmother in a grey dress inside an oval frame had come to hang from the same nail. Later someone in the family said the frame would look pretty above her table with the washbasin.

Take it, Grandmother said.

After that the room was snow-white and regal. The ceiling was high and white, the window was lower and higher than normal windows (House Samuel was indeed a castle!) with unpainted wooden shutters that opened to the outside. Inside there were white curtains that fell like milk. The bed linen was also white. At a time when the whole world had discovered duvets and bedding could be bought in sets, gaudy sets with dainty patterns in every possible shade of disappointment, Grandmother kept her linen cupboard white. Bed linen crackled like the paper wrapped around expensive soap and pillows smelled like church perfume, like a garden inside a drawer. It was the smell of wealth and age, no young family with speckled carpets and blinds could produce such a smell. In the middle of the room hung a single light bulb, too high and with a too-small lampshade, but still white.

The bed was wider than a single bed and soft. There were no blankets, only sheets and a down thing covered in starched white fabric. In winter there was a throw made of dassie skins. How I, the child whose flesh crawled for everything, could make myself at home under forty murdered little animals, I don't know. Perhaps somewhere in my arsenal there was a book with illustrations of knights or noblemen wrapped in furs, it's still a puzzle. Perhaps it was part of the rituals of this room, the absence of rules or time, the warm milk with late-night scones, the secret breakfast while others have to go and eat in the kitchen, Grandmother bringing me grown-up magazines so I can discover fashion while other boys dream of revolvers, lying in bed even when you are awake and the sun is shining; here there is no school, sports days or parents with weekend plans.

This room remains the most perfect space in which I have ever found myself. The emptiness, the white, the simplicity, the slight echo, a footstep on a carpetless surface, all of this I recreate wherever I go. There have been many derailments in my homes, as taste and fancy evolve: patterns, colours, draperies, unnecessary furniture, standing lamps from expensive shops, cushions embellished and embroidered, monsters from every era or style appearing around me, but when sanity returns I return to white and empty. I walk through museums and galleries and gaze at the high ceilings, the emptiness between the artworks and the halls delivered from all furniture.

I sit upright. There are noises outside. A warm night wind rustles everything that can be rustled. I am without fear, in this room there are no nightmares and no sleepwalking, just a silver glow through an open window. I get out of bed and kneel before the low windowsill. I see Big Tree One, the trees down the slope, the nasturtiums, the fence before the vineyard, the beginning of the vineyard path and the far curtain of Donkiebos.

One of the shutters hasn't been fastened, I push it open and reach out to fasten the little black hook. I see how the ground outside changes colour, light grey, light blue, bright blue, electric blue. I look up, everything, everything is blue. Every thing, every tree, every plant is blue and each peak glowing, crowned in glass blue. Every object I know, every growing thing, every stone-hard dead thing, each is etched, cut out and dipped in glitter, each moves to the foreground, each apart, but nothing comes closer. The sky is blue and there is a moon, brighter than possible, it's not a full moon, it's an oval that burns like a still white fire. But the sky, the air and everything below it are blue.

The moment was unreal, almost in bad taste, like a Christmas card with minute lights or a tune. Thanks to small batteries, lights and tunes disappear, but this gleaming, living forest didn't grow dim, it was there in front of me and I didn't want to look away. Eventually I fell asleep at the windowsill and woke up the next morning with a deep groove in my cheek.

I had never seen such a thing before, and have never seen it since. Much later I read about a Blue Moon, a kind of full moon that seems blue-ish because of a unique dust in the atmosphere, but that's not what happened that night.

Many years later, *my* blue made an appearance at an unexpected place. As a music student I spent more time with the drama students than in my own practice room. On the stage of the HB Thom theatre in Stellenbosch I started experimenting with songs and short stories, so much so that Emile Aucamp, technical head of the drama department, decided to teach me about stage lighting. For one of my very first public efforts I wanted a slow, soft version of the song 'Cabaret', sung without any front lighting; I wanted to hold a lit cigarette in a pool of intense blue light. Emile hung the light, focused it and put in a double blue lighting gel. I went and stood on my spot and was lost for words, I could see my hands and arms glowing in an unnatural, magical blue beam of light, I could touch it and see it move on my skin.

Blue is not a colour I want to wear or decorate with, but an object or being dipped in a glow, the carrier of an unreal blue light, that is what I keep longing for – also the room and the tall window and the shutters and the freedom – but, above all, inexplicably, unrestrainedly, insatiably, the blue!

Only recently have I come to understand (or admit) that I still try to recreate that moment at the windowsill every time I step onto a stage. After more than 6 000 performances I realise that this is how every show begins: as soon as the doors of the auditorium open and the audience enters, there are blue shafts of light over the position of each musician, often also over the instruments, décor and my microphone on its stand. Anyone who has attended more than one of my performances can testify to this. It is one of the constants in my existence, me waiting, panic-stricken, in the wings for the house lights to dim, for the musicians to walk into their blue light, hearing the first refrains and seeing the blue light intensify until everyone begins to glow with their own crown. Only then do I take my first step and relax almost immediately, only when the people with whom I have worked and joked for years transform before my eyes into the beings who fifty years ago on a blue night in Wellington signalled to me, Welcome here, whether you want to or not, this is where you belong.

More Shutters

My father was restless his entire life: he could socialise like no-body else, remember more jokes than anyone, was the first to help when there was need, but he had an itch, always making plans to build a better life, always trapped by his own decisions. For decades now I have waged a war against insomnia, the ghost that likes to rob me of my strength and make me feel ages old, and when I roam about my home at night I remember how, as a young child, I saw my father sitting: I was always on my way to the fridge for a midnight meal, he was always sitting at the table with his head in his hands. I thought he was also hungry; now I know he was desperate, at war with himself and his circumstances.

Is it hereditary? I have created an entirely different life, almost the exact opposite of my father's, but I am constantly wrestling with my world, too often I curse my small life, I look at other artists, read about other occupations, stare at acquaintances who travel easily, then call myself pathetic, provincial, disappointing.

A long time ago someone said that people who always talk about themselves or announce everything they plan on doing, never manage to do anything. Those who earn international success don't sit on a chair and discuss desires, they get on an airplane and land next to the rainbow; those who manage to emigrate seldom say a word, one morning they're just gone; those brave enough to start a new career don't lie awake for twenty years, they run through the flames while they are young and strong, quickly and quietly. Maybe that is the truth, maybe that's the reason for all my trauma and nothingness: I announce everything. Have I told you? I am going there for three weeks, I decided to tackle the new production like this, no, I can't join you, I am meeting so and so, oh, have I mentioned that I'm only eating organically now?

And then everything does happen, I have already told the whole world, but with trauma and panic and fury and impatience and pain and fanfare and sweat and explosions. And then I quickly skip off back to the small life, lock the door, here I am again, having learnt nothing.

My grandmother seldom announced anything. Why couldn't I have inherited this ability? She was a master of surprise. She could astonish you without the least effort. Were her days just too full to talk about tomorrow? Did things just keep on happening suddenly or was there a secret notebook?

It was during a gathering or one of the family's short visits or one of my solo holidays, I can't remember. Early one morning I walk into the kitchen. Grandmother and two strange women are sitting at the table. It smells like ten dogs have just been given a bath in a room without windows.

Good morning, Grandmother, I say, What's that smell?

Say hello to Piggy, says Grandmother.

In an enamel bowl in the middle of the table is a pig's head. I shudder like someone doing a naughty dance. The women laugh.

The lamb's head is already in the pot, says Grandmother. That's what smells so bad, but it will go away soon, we'll add the nice curry then the whole house will smell like a banquet.

Grandmother and the two women each sit before a plank with a rubbery pink organ and a sharp knife. They scrape the rubber. It looks like hair with dandruff that's falling onto the plank. I do another dance. The women laugh again.

Tomorrow afternoon I'll give you a slice of fresh bread and thin slices of favourite, says Grandmother.

What's favourite? I ask.

Brawn! says Grandmother, Didn't you ask yesterday when we were going to have brawn again?

It was a favourite. A jelly with curry and bits of meat-pie filling, set in the shape of a small loaf. Grandmother always cut it into thin slices and laid them out in rows on the big oval platter. Delicious, delicious. For a quick treat on thick slices of bread, for eating at the table with potato salad and lots of parsley.

Why is the pig in the bowl? I ask.

Now where do you think the brawn meat comes from? laughs
Grandmother.

I swallow hard.

I'm going to say good morning to Grandfather, I say.

Out the back door, across the lawn, at the fence full of peels I turn
left. Here the hard ground started to become a lawn, there was a
row of trees, to the left of the trees was the small hall, to the right
of the trees a driveway, two lines of cement that led to a garage, to
the right of the garage the big neat house. This house's name was
Clairvaux and it was originally inhabited by Rev Andrew Murray;
in Grandmother's time it was inhabited by Dr Johan van der
Merwe. Like the social worker girls Dr Johan was never around,
the house was always shuttered.

What we could see from Samuel was the back of Clairvaux, all
the ordinariness of a back door with everything happening on
either side. The front was thus never seen except by inhabitants
or visitors. And those of us who skulked. I sneak past the garage,
through the small entrance to the front garden. Here the shutters
began. Shutters from just below the eaves down to the ground.
Like Boudoir biscuits stuck all the way around a square cake the
shutters went along the side, the front, and the other side of the
long house, all evenly spaced. A low, narrow porch stretched
along the entire front of the house – was it a wooden porch? I
remember long, narrow planks. The porch roof rested on thin
pillars, metal, wood? Again I remember wood. And fine detail

where it met the roof, not latticework and curls like the Victorians preferred, a more exotic block motif as if from the East.

Scores of people would give you another description, but I last saw the house more than forty years ago and no picture seems to exist, I abide entirely by my own experience.

From the porch the fine lawn stretched downwards to a green end, a wall of lush trees and shrubs. I decided it was a vlei, a small vlei for dramatic visits. I always lay down just below the porch and rolled down to the bottom of the hill. Not because it was fun, but because other children were always jumping about, doing cartwheels, somersaults and handstands, running or crawling, all activities rejected by my young body, and I felt I should make my contribution to childhood. Rolling upset me the least.

So I fulfil my role on the morning of the pig's head. I lie on my stomach and look up at the house. This long house with its closed shutters and regularly spaced, thin pillars, neatly placed on its green hill, fascinated me: the delicacy, the symmetry, the elegance. I felt it was part of a story that all children should know but were never told.

There was never a desire to open anything, to know which shutters hid doors or windows, to look inside. There was something charming about the shutters themselves, the rough feel of the old wood, the greyness of each slat, the smell of the oil with which they had been painted long ago. I wanted to be outside, locked out, or inside, locked up. I imagined the whole house consisted of one room, so big you would never need the outside again. I never made a sound, when other children were around I kept shushing them. Perhaps Dr Johan was inside, he wouldn't be in the mood for us and our noise.

Since then I have had the privilege to visit a few other houses with ceiling-height shutters; the feel and the smell are always the same, immediately I am back on the sloping lawn.

Someone moves on the porch. I get a fright and sit upright. Nobody ever said whether we were allowed here or not, and I've always been the most cautious pigeon in the park, flapping and panicked after every sudden movement. I shuffle backwards, there is a shrub behind me in which I can disappear. But now the porch is empty again.

Then a woman laughs. It's a loud laugh, but it sounds far away, like when a radio is playing in another room. Then a man laughs, also far away. I shuffle right up to the shrub. They appear at the same time, twenty, more even, the whole length of the porch, soft as tissue against the light, slightly transparent, a painting in apricot, cream, rose, light green, light grey, light blue. They are tall and slender, each with a cigarette or a cocktail glass, the kind with stems, Grandmother uses them for fruit salad.

The shutters are gone, the house is open, it is one big room with fans on the ceiling and palms in big pots. Men in bow-ties carry trays, someone plays the piano, someone sits on the arm of a big armchair. I look at their hair: all of them, men and women, have pitch-black hair, smooth and slicked back, there isn't a curl or a fringe. Women wear bands with small stones around their heads, others have tied their scarves in such a way that the ends hang down their backs. The dresses are all cut straight to just above the ankles, the shoes have low heels and straps across the instep. Everyone wears long strings of beads around their necks, some hanging down the front, others down the back. The men have small moustaches and dark lashes. All of them, men and women, are gorgeous, are happy, they touch each other often and keep on laughing.

It will be years before I know anything about Gatsby, flappers, bootlegging or the Charleston, but it is here, right in front of me, on a porch in Wellington. A few are dancing, they shuffle their feet and move their straight arms backwards and forwards. I straighten my own arms and try to copy the movements. Just a little.

Mmm, says a voice. Not Mmm for *This is nice* but Mmm for *I see*. The voice is deep and in a circle around me. It is a new voice, but I know it's The Prince.

Grandfather appears next to the house.

Grandmother says there might be a grandchild on the lawn here, he says.

The shutters are closed, the slender people are gone, the porch is dead. Grandfather coughs.

If there is such a person here, he should follow me home for breakfast, he says, We are eating in the front room, the kitchen is going to reek for a while still.

I walk behind Grandfather back to House Samuel.

If I were you, I wouldn't tell anyone anything just yet, he says. In that house they study the Bible, nobody is ready yet for tales about dancing.

He coughs again.

The Palace Of Future Revelations

A narrow untarred road, rock hard, curled around House Samuel up to where guests parked their cars under Big Tree Two. Out the front door, down a few steps, across the narrow dirt road, up to the edge of a lawn as big as an athletics field – this is how you walked to the strip: a straight line of cement had been laid along the entire length of the lawn. On the other side, directly opposite the front door of Samuel, was the front door of The Palace Of Future Revelations.

This building was long, horrible and drab, a blemish from the middle of the twentieth century, a time when modern wasn't modern everywhere yet. Here more students were housed and here lived my grandmother's good friend, Auntie Gee. She was the cook, maybe also matron, of Friedenheim, that's what that long horribleness was called.

In all the years that I visited there, I never – as with House Samuel –

saw a single student, not *one* girl. It was only Auntie Gee and the vast, vast silence. There was a rectangular entrance hall. The front door consisted of double glass panels with wooden frames and white, slightly translucent curtains, like those that stretched across millions of glass doors in the sixties and seventies. Similar panels stood guard on either side of the front door, the whole breadth of the entrance hall. Above each panel (or long window) was open glass that let in the afternoon sun.

Were you to enter, close the front door and turn around, in front of you there would be another row of glass panels, also with wooden frames and double doors, that led to the dining hall. To your right there was another glass door, also covered in white curtains, that led to a hallway and Auntie Gee's flat; maybe there were more.

To your left was a staircase, one of those that you can walk underneath, a wide staircase with steel railings, handrails of dark-brown plastic and millions of tiny biscuit-coloured mosaic tiles. These tiles I recognised the first time I saw them; in my young life there had already been enough courtyards, school staircases and hospital foyers covered in these little clay scales to make me wonder. Who would choose such a thing? Who would manufacture such a thing? How long was it going to stay?

You had to walk through the dining hall to find the kitchen and Auntie Gee. Like most spaces for a child, this dining hall was an especially big room, always dusky, with rows of abandoned tables and chairs. Here hung thick, long, closed curtains, different from any other curtains from that era. A few times, when the dining hall felt less unsafe, I went to touch those curtains. They were smooth, like thin leather, and unfamiliar, almost futuristic; I was in the belly of a deserted vehicle, a ship without a crew.

The kitchen was an explosion of light and possibilities, a long room with rows of steel tables, the steel tables I would later discover in other professional kitchens and would eventually want my whole life: operating tables ready for every possible banquet. In this kitchen hundreds of dishes could be prepared, hordes could be entertained from here, here rows upon rows of trays could stand ready to serve throngs of privileged people, out of breath after hours of dancing.

Do they dance here a lot? I asked once.

Silly child, Auntie Gee laughed, It's a Christian college!

Since not one girl was ever in sight, there was never any cooking in my hundreds of visits. But there was always food, cloths were lifted from plates, lids were lifted from tins, upside-down plates were lifted from platters and I was fed. Auntie Gee laughed and I ate.

If people say you're a fat little boy, don't mind them, she said. They know nothing, your grandmother loves you terribly!

On one side of the kitchen there were windows, tall windows that overlooked a thicket, the back yard, if a palace disguised as a half-modern institute had a back yard. It was green and picturesque. Once or twice for a fleeting moment there would be dozens of people under the trees, deck chairs, young girls with ribbons in their hair, older women with straw hats and long dresses in light pink and light yellow, men with narrow moustaches and wrinkled white suits, some with umbrellas, others with books, smallish tables with jelly towers and cut cakes. These moments were so completely real – I could hear them laugh – but passed too quickly; I wanted to call Auntie Gee and ask her about them. Eventually, without afterthought or a definite decision, I just kept quiet about it.

There were other moments. Once, Auntie Gee was standing bowed at one of the long tables with yellowed sheets of paper, searching for a rusk recipe that she'd promised my grandmother, when the kitchen's swing doors (were these swing doors before?) suddenly swung open and two waiters with white gloves and black uniforms, luxuriously decorated with red braid, stormed into the kitchen and threw their silver trays onto the steel tables. They immediately went back through the swing doors. For a few seconds I could see the dining hall was lit in gold, with heavy bunches of fairy lights hanging from the ceiling. (Until that moment in my life I had not once heard the word 'chandelier'.) I had already had enough music lessons to know it was a waltz that was being played. Just before the swing doors closed, I saw the skirt of a light-blue crinoline twirl, a thousand ruffles of a thousand petticoats flashed in white. Then everything was quiet.

Here it is, said Auntie Gee, Buttermilk rusks with lemon peel.

A few months later, the next time I visited, there was another moment. This time two other waiters bumped open the swing doors. They put down trays with half-full glasses, quickly took a few gulps and rushed back. A soldier with a chest full of medals lifted a girl off her feet and spun her round. The jewels in her hair glittered in the light of the chandelier. I looked around. Auntie Gee and my grandmother were peeling peaches.

It's so nice to cook for Christmas! Grandmother said, Everything just tastes better!

There was one time that the kitchen was completely busy. It was the last Sunday of a holiday and the girls would begin to return that afternoon for the new semester. My parents would come and fetch me after my umpteenth holiday at my grandmother's. Auntie Gee and her helpers were making hundreds of hot dogs.

Most of the girls come from far away, Auntie Gee said, They will be hungry, that's not a proper plate of food, but who gets upset over a vienna?

In between the trays of buttered buns there were big metal servers full of strings of vienna sausages. These viennas would later be cut and thrown in pots of boiling water before being folded into the buns with mustard and tomato sauce. I stood on top of a steel table and devoured a vienna every time someone turned their back. The pop of the skin was more beautiful than any music.

Auntie Gee roared with laughter.

We don't see anything! Take another one!

It was here, in Friedenheim, ordinary and extraordinary, horrible and fantastic, that I would learn of big and of small, here so many images of what I would later learn were shown to me for the first time; only after many years would I realise it and remember, but the theme of my entire life, the reason for my eternal discomfort, was handed to me here. An entrance hall that led to Auntie Gee's tiny flat – a whole existence in three small rooms, every day waiting for the afternoon sun and a nap in an easy chair – also led to a dormant dining hall, sometimes grey and inexplicable, sometimes golden, full of immortal dancers and a never-ending waltz, also led to a hostel kitchen, sometimes homely and fun, sometimes in deadly routine, sometimes in service of a royal ball.

Childhood or adulthood, living small or achieving big, standing back or triumphing, acceptance or rebellion, contentment or disappointment, gratitude or thirst, humiliation or pride, peace or commotion, these opposites would tear me in two, for decades and decades.

I was still in primary school when Grandmother and Grandfather announced that they had to move out of Samuel. Grandfather had been transferred to another campus. It was just before Christmas. I didn't know if it would be our last visit there. I walked along the cement strip for an afternoon with Auntie Gee. The building was quieter than ever. I crossed the hallway and pushed open her flat's front door. She was asleep in the easy chair. I went back to the entrance hall. Unsure of what to do, I stood and looked at the front door. Rays of sunshine fell on me through the upper pane. I looked down at my two fat, shapeless primary-school legs. And my two puffy hands, the hands that a high-school teacher would call 'dough claws' a few years later and that an unloved journalist would describe as 'granny hands'. There was a sound, an intake of breath from underneath the earth, a thousand-year-old rustling; at my right the staircase with its clay scales began to move, elegantly and slowly it began lifting from the centre. The stairs disappeared; like a monster curling its back, without breaking away at the bottom or losing a single tile, it formed a perfect arch, glowing in the sun, the wing of a giant dragon or a being that I would never be able to describe. Then there was a sigh, deep and almost inaudible; the staircase returned to its original shape and I remained standing with the sun on my legs and hands, and I knew something inexplicable, alive and vast, would always be with me.

The Palace Of Future Revelations never revealed itself to me again, I have no knowledge of its ever being shown again in any form to another child.

More than forty years later I went back to House Samuel for a television interview. Afterwards I realised that I hadn't once looked in the direction of Auntie Gee's hostel. The lawn was gone and so was the strip. I asked my family if they could remember the name of the building, but no one could; only later did my one cousin remember it as Friedenheim. I went and searched for it on the internet, it was nowhere to be found, not even on the college's website or on Google's satellite pictures. Maybe others can find it, maybe it is still full of girls, but to me it's gone.

The Heavy Castle

It is the middle of the night and I am in the middle of The Five Holes Of The Constant Chord. Only a few steps further and I can lean the bicycle against the wall. I hear my mother's voice over the chord.

Here he comes, she says.

I don't know why I can hear her, I don't know why I can hear the chord, I am sleeping. I was never afraid of the dark, only of sleeping. It came so seldom, it remained a stranger. Read, pray, turn off the light, lie and lie and lie until you have called up all the voices, have chewed over all the stories, until hunger has come and gone, until exhaustion makes you fall into a quiet well, just long enough so you will believe tomorrow that you slept. The Real Sleep came to make trouble two, three times a week, you fought and you lost, you were motionless for a few hours and then the chord came calling.

During the day, The Five Holes Of The Constant Chord was

our entrance hall. A front door, my parents' bedroom door, my bedroom door, the living-room door and the beginning of a short hallway met to form this rectangle. The floor was quiet and hard, unlike the rest of the house's noisy wooden floors. Tiles? Stone? Cement? Ancient ice? The hardest wood on earth? I don't know. The front door was always closed, the other doors were open, the hallway gaping. On chosen nights these five holes began to hum, five wind directions met here and a soft, deep chord was formed. Like voices in a choir that never ran out of breath this chord called to me; sleeping I lifted my blanket and got out of bed. I reached out my hand until I could feel the bicycle. This bicycle only existed in the dark, a silver bicycle, only just visible, with a thin frame, no pedals, no chain; the wheels turned when I held the handles and walked alongside it. Slowly I began moving from my room to The Five Holes Of The Constant Chord.

The Heavy Castle appeared by itself. From my middle to just above my head, that was the height of the castle, but higher at night, because it was balanced on the bicycle's two handlebars, wobbly like a jelly tower. And heavy, I had to use all my strength to make the bicycle move. There wasn't an extra hand to stabilise the castle, instinctively I knew there was only one way to protect my load: worry. Enough worry would keep the castle upright.

Where the order had come from was unclear, but night after night I had to get The Heavy Castle to its destination. Where that was I never really knew; as soon as I reached the end of The Five Holes Of The Constant Chord, I left the bicycle against the wall, I had to go and tell my parents.

Hunnunnkinnehunnelillewinnefunne, I mumbled.

I rub my hands, repeatedly and anxiously. I have to convince my father and mother that I have accomplished my task.

Kinnekinnehunnedinnewinnekinnekinne.

The worry won't go away. I rub my hands. Rub them, rub them.

Just help him back, says my mother, Don't let him wake up, then he'll start crying again.

My father comes out of the room, he puts his hands on my shoulders and turns me around.

It's okay, he says, Everything is okay.

I sleep, but I hear everything. I get back into bed, my father pulls the blanket over me. I hope they are happy, I hope everyone is happy, The Heavy Castle is on the opposite side, I hope the Real Sleep is happy, now he can stay away again, he makes me so tired.

After a night like that I look at the four doors in the morning, they hang in their frames like any other doors, they give nothing away. I walk to the hallway, so short, only two metres, then turn right, here are another four metres, on the left-hand side are the doors to the toilet and bathroom, now the floor becomes soft wood, here is the dining room and then the ugly kitchen. The kitchen is dark, I tell myself, because it is the locomotive, here coals are shovelled into the furnace, one of these days we will have enough steam to leave.

By any measure I am now a fat boy and we live in Porterville, right in the middle of town in a street parallel to the high street. Our house is a rolled-up train. Go inside, look to the right, my room, middle, entrance hall, left, parents' room, turn right, toilet, bathroom, dining room, kitchen, turn right, back porch, turn right, into another room, does my brother sleep here? Right, living room. Curled up in a spiral, our train, where in the world would you find another house like this?

Stand on the back porch: now you are looking at a biggish lawn, to the left is a lush tree, if I had to sketch it, it would be an avocado tree full of loquats, to the right is a massive fig tree, behind it, the garage. Where the lawn ends, tarred poles keep a dark wooden fence upright. Behind the fence is more yard, but it is wild, there are piles of planks and tall weeds with prickly leaves. A few tomato plants climb up a wooden frame, the beginnings of a vegetable garden, but my father is busy, he works long hours at the town's garage, he helps everywhere a strong hand is needed and sings in the church choir. (At the top of his voice! Two years later a new organist is brave enough to ask him to leave the gallery. After that he sings even louder, below among the congregation. At what age is a child allowed to sit by himself?)

My mother is also busy, she has to rearrange the train, a new baby is on its way, the third one.

I often stand underneath the fig tree. It's nice, the smell and taste of a sun-ripened fig. And the shade underneath the tree. It is one of my few pleasures. I am unhappy here, I do not belong in this house, I am anxious and rebellious, every day I feel less at home and I show this in every possible way; 'a difficult child' is the quiet consensus of guests and acquaintances. And my family has to live and last, they don't have the time or energy for my growing unhappiness.

My stomach begins to ache, but I eat my fifth fig. Here I'm going to shed many tears, an ocean of salt water will spill from my eyes, what else can I do? Only when this town is washed away in the flood of a child's sorrow, only then might another soldier appear.

Left, Right, Across

If you stood on our front porch and looked at the street, there was a semi-detached house on your left-hand side. Someone must have lived in the half closest to us, I remember the back yard and the dilapidated door of the enclosed porch, but there is no memory of a face or a name. In the other half there lived a woman with a cockatoo, two full-grown sons and a display cabinet full of christening cakes. I visited here practically every day: there was always a plate of shop biscuits on the kitchen table and the elder son fascinated me. He lived in the front bedroom like it was a separate house. The walls were covered from floor to ceiling in movie posters, pictures from magazines – mostly of cars, horses and girls in bikinis – and his own sketches. He wore a leather jacket and his one shoe had a thicker sole than the other. He seldom left the house and drew with a pencil or a ballpoint pen on every piece of paper he could lay his hands on, cars, horses and girls in bikinis. He smoked cigarettes and was friendly, he would talk to me for hours as though we were the same age. The other son was a phantom, he appeared and disappeared, sometimes yanked open the bedroom door looking for a shirt or a jersey, never noticed anyone. There was also a daughter, older than the brothers, a thin woman with pitch-black hair, in another story she was a slender, exhausted Spanish dancer. She was married to a farmer, a man with blond curls, canvas shoes and tiny shorts in light pink or light yellow. It always looked like she wanted to sleep and he was on his way to the beach, but they had to farm and every second day they delivered hundreds of eggs in town without a smile.

Next to the semi was a smallish hall with a pretty, old-fashioned front, this was the library. Apart from Grandmother's house in Wellington, it was the best place in the universe. Thousands of books, each neatly wrapped in thick plastic, were waiting. There was a section for children and one for adults. I read everything, Verna Vels, Astrid Lindgren, Enid Blyton, Beatrix Potter and Lewis Carroll. In an era when rules, no matter how stupid or repressive, were frantically implemented by anyone with the least drop of authority, a woman had been sent by the angels to run this library. She allowed me to look where I wanted, no book in the adult section was out of bounds; in this lovely temple of paper I could read as much as I wanted, I could take home as many as I wanted.

Next door was the church, the biggest and most dramatic landmark in town. Here I was confirmed as the town's music boy. At one stage I started playing the recorder, a sound that still upsets me, but it was something new, a sidestep in my search for musical deliverance. Everything except the sound excited me: two recorders, brand new in their cases, one a soprano in shiny brown wood, the other a cream-coloured alto. At every special occasion I was next to the organ in the gallery, sometimes with the church choir, sometimes with the school choir, sometimes on my own. I was crazy about the excitement of a performance, all the people, the happy chaos of a new piece and the hope that somewhere in the air my terrible solo would transform into something beautiful. The fear was still minor.

If you stood on our front porch and looked towards the street, there was a dairy on your right-hand side, a small white building without cows, but with lots of milk. There were rows of buckets and primitive machines, a metal counter, a shelf with loaves of farm bread and two friendly men. They chatted like there were no problems in the world, while before your eyes glass bottles were filled with foaming milk and sealed with silver foil tops. I went inside only once, the smell was dreadful. Afterwards my mother sent me every second day, I stood on the white building's porch, one man rolled his eyes, the other laughed and brought me a bottle and a loaf.

On the next corner was a park with a metal frame without swings, a roundabout and brown grass as unhealthy as the back of a mangy dog. Sometimes there was an expressionless nanny with an expressionless child, round and round on the roundabout until it stopped, no attempt at another go, then their disappearance and the park was empty for days on end.

Across from the park was the cinema, a shabby white building straight out of a classic thriller. This theatre belonged to a foreigner in Piketberg and every Friday evening the threadbare oasis presented a feature film. Westerns, musicals and Afrikaans weepies were the three categories. We didn't even bother finding out what was showing, we just arrived, mostly the town's children;

few adults would brave the decay. Seats were decrepit, covered in ripped red velvet through which wads of stuffing bulged. There was a rush for seats as far to the back as possible – a big hole in the wall underneath the screen let in an icy wind and those in the front rows froze. Above was a big gallery and here the coloured people sat. They talked, yelled out comments, sang and complained loudly when the story wasn't going as wished. Every now and then a prim Shhh! rose from the seats below, then it rained rubbish from above, we were showered in cooldrink cans, beer cans and clumps of sweet wrappers. A full-scale war broke out every time the film came to an abrupt end because the foreigner had forgotten again to send all the reels. Seats were ripped out, lights were smashed and handrails were used to attack the remaining windowpanes. Despite all the violence we turned up every time the cinema opened its tired doors, we were there for the darkness. As soon as the short newsreel started, all the lights were dimmed and then we grabbed. We held hands with whoever landed next to us. I always made sure I ended up next to my best friend, a lovely farm boy. On my other side was a girl, my date for the evening. We began dating hideously early – each Friday by break you found out who was going to the cinema and then there were wild pairings. This arrangement ended as soon as the evening's film did, but I would remember my friend's hand the whole week.

Across from the cinema there was a side street, here you walked past two houses on your left and then suddenly there was shrubbery on both sides of the road. To the right was the town garden, a spacious square with shrubs, fruit trees, rose bushes and metal arches heavy with creepers, which bordered the mangy park. To the left was an imposing house in a lush garden. One afternoon a week I anxiously pushed open the garden gate on my way to my piano lesson. Here I was taught to say Ma'am, not Aunt or Miss. My music teacher was an older lady from a respected family, her son excelled at rugby or airplanes. The front door swallowed you reluctantly and then spat you out in a living room with a brown grand piano and walls covered in dull Pierneef paintings. Here Ma'am killed my love for music, page by page. My pieces were simple, one-note melodies with an arpeggio accompaniment, but nothing was right, too fast, too slow, too messy, too monotonous, too loud, too soft. Child, did you practise?! On top of the piano, to the left of the sheet music, was a porcelain bowl with boiled sweets, these sweets were there as a reward for excellence, but in all the months, years or centuries that I went there, no sweet was ever offered, not to me or any other pupil; the sweets remained untouched like pebbles on an unvisited grave. I fantasised about how I would break in at night, colour in each horrible painting with the brightest crayons in existence and then devour the contents of the porcelain bowl. As with all places that damage you, I remember every detail of that house, each Persian carpet, each crystal vase, the growling dog, the varnished doorframes, the low ceiling, the dead acoustics. At the end of every lesson I fled to a place with no agenda.

If you stood on our front porch and looked towards the street, you were also looking at the old-age home, a broad, low building, sometimes a dull yellow, sometimes a dull blue, surrounded by a straggly garden. The front door was at the corner of the building and immediately upon entry the building divided itself into two corridors: one stretched out in front of you, one immediately turned right. The walls were covered in thick, custard-coloured enamel paint, the floors in custard-coloured hospital plastic. Two wooden handrails ran the full length of both corridors, every day a crowd of ballerinas clutched at these, stretching sore muscles for a final *Swan Lake*.

The corridor before you led to the matron's office, the lounge, dining room, sun lounge and kitchen. I wandered through these spaces, frightened by the otherness of old age, relieved by the lack of judgement or expectation; here they smiled at me or ignored me, nobody raised a questioning eyebrow, nobody raised a voice in command, nobody raised a hand in argument. I was like a stray cat, some were glad to see me, others didn't care.

Would you like some juice? a nurse asked.

No, thank you, I said.

I knew it would be in a glass with an orange pattern and too many scratch marks.

A biscuit? the cook asked.

No, thank you, I said.

But I can see you like biscuits, look at those cheeks! the cook laughed.

Of course I like biscuits, I thought, I can eat twenty. I can eat myself sick and then well again. But here you get a biscuit on a plastic plate, a listless red plate with too many scratch marks.

The people who could transport me, those who could effortlessly call up excitement, they were all old, older than adults, older than Ma'am, they were old people, full of revelations, and afterwards still full of secrets. They were irrepressible and timeless and inspired like Grandmother. In the building across from our home they were slow and frail, sometimes cranky and curt, always toying with my thoughts, unwilling to let me relax. I envied them their serenity, their closed eyes in the afternoon sun, the skinny legs under crocheted blankets; at the same time I was frightened of their hands, the crooked fingers and the blue veins, also the smell in the corridor leading to the bedrooms and the sickbay. When I wasn't there I missed the things they knew and were sometimes prepared to share, the sudden explosions of energy and the screamingly funny moments of silliness, also the freedom of people who hardly feared anything any more. But when I was there I shuddered at the crumbs on a lap or the droplet on a chin, uneasy in the presence of decay.

But I couldn't stay away. In my family there was a quiet belief that you had to honour your elders and catch those who stumbled. You will need others in your own unsteady days, will the mighty ones who have to send your saviours know of your actions? Oversimplifying, old-fashioned, even neurotic to walk around with such a conviction – say what you like, I went to visit and still do. Across the road, among the wise, however talkative or quiet, a power gathers at which I must suckle. Without it all the little devils, struggles, lust, blood, sweat, spit, prophets, skeletons and doubt are just too much to bear.

Susie & Kit

Mother, how long have Aunt Susie and Aunt Kit lived here?

For much longer than we've been on earth, why are you asking this now?

I'm just asking.

A short distance from our home, in the same side street as the dairy, lived two aunts, no other word would do, they were aunts: Aunt Susie, tall and thin, and Aunt Kit, short and stout. Their house was small and right on the road, there was a front garden as broad as a brushstroke, full of fine grass and lacy flowers, the minute, almost-translucent flowers that can't be planted but only sprout – each in a different colour – in the vicinity of an absolutely unique presence or shelter. Nowhere else could you have as nice a time as here, here you were cherished and fed, here you were never bothered. Most of the townspeople never even noticed this house, it was only meant for a few.

One day, when the two aunts were talking, standing in front of a window, their bodies etched against the sharp morning light, I realised with a slight shock that they had the same shape as The Stoepsusters. No one knew if these two were in fact sisters, but could Bora and Becca have changed their names and followed me here? Were they so overcome with guilt that they had to supply all the sweets here as well? Shouldn't they rather be helping me to escape this ball of baby fat?

My mother's answer helped me to relax: I could just visit. And I did. As often as possible.

Imagine a doll's house starts to grow, wallpaper rips open, paint peels in places, here and there a teacup or a milk jug falls off a table and loses an ear, eventually it is big enough to step inside. Two characters leave a very old story and enter through the back door, they are now your hostesses, here for no other reason than to make you feel at home. That's how it was at Aunt Susie and Aunt Kit's. For the rest of my life, this is the kind of memory I keep returning to, a lovely landing on a soft mattress.

Everything inside the house was a little bit worn, every cupboard slightly skew, every table tilted, every door too loose in its frame, carpets' patterns fading, aprons patched many times, boots long since worn through, each of the embroidered shawls in front of the windows missing a few threads, portraits long since glassless. Two small bedrooms on either side of the front door, no electricity here, lopsided candles in copper candleholders, short passage full of ferns, cluttered living room, kitchen, pantry, back porch. No bathroom, just a tap and two basins in a small room behind the pantry, no toilet – a stone path led to a wooden outhouse in a bed of lavender. Everything combined to form a picture that time and again took my breath away, so charming I almost didn't want to believe it; no stylist on a film set could have created it, something like this was the result of a long life and the perfect balance between true poverty and wealth.

And there was wealth. In the middle of the kitchen was a small, square wooden table with two chairs. Two more chairs were brought in from the back porch for guests. The table was always set, two plates, two forks, two napkins, two bowls, two spoons, a custard jug draped with a doily clinking with red glass beads. A thin net with embroidered flowers covered everything. In this house pudding was served twice a day: except for breakfast, no meal was finished before a dessert appeared. Sometimes a serving of vinegar pudding, sometimes a spoonful of sago, sometimes a fresh apricot, sometimes a bottled peach, always with a blanket of custard. Fruitcake, gingerbread, banana bread, raisin bread, grape tart, gooseberry tart, milk tart, poached quince, baked apples, fresh figs, preserved oranges, from the pantry, from a tiny ice-box, from behind a curtain, from a painted tin, from behind the scarecrow, from everywhere sweet things appeared and were served in tiny portions. (Just a taste, as soon as gratitude comes, you're done!)

No muscled valet, no marble step, no golden tassel, no strange hand with fragrant oils, no shiny motor car, no heavy diamond, no sip of an award-winning wine, no take-off in a private jet, nothing comes close to the riches I experienced in this tiny house. Even without pudding, in the living room with a cup of tea and a plain biscuit, among decades' worth of collector's pieces, beheaded porcelain princesses, lace and paper fans, an antique Chinese parasol and a fringed lamp on top of two carved wooden snakes, the aunts told such stories and evoked such images that I couldn't believe we were sitting in a town filled with the ordinariness of a post office, a hair salon or a police station. In rare moments of silence their worn-in shoes (Aunt Susie's made of thin squares of leather or covered in fabrics from a faraway land, Aunt Kit's decorated with beadwork or painted by hand) or their jewellery (a big sleeping face hanging from a ribbon round a neck or a chorus of silver dancing girls around an arm) told another tale. I couldn't believe that I ever had to walk down an ordinary street again or wear shorts or live through a meal that ended without pudding.

Exhausting detail, daily rituals, so the favour of kings is won. I haul this wealth from a place that few ever knew, a small, small house on a long, narrow erf in the middle of Porterville.

Back to Malmesbury

We have a new baby brother, his name is Erik and he is happier than a garden gnome. He balls his fists and kicks and laughs as if he already understands all the jokes. Father and Mother are worn out, their third son will never let them sleep again, he parties and plans adventures.

Suddenly Erik is ill, some child thing, that's what I gather. He cannot stay at home, the illness is too contagious, he's under quarantine in Malmesbury's hospital. We are forlorn, the house feels forsaken, the kitchen is darker than ever, at night I push the castle on the bicycle, my arms hurt, my load becomes heavier and heavier.

Every afternoon Father leaves work early, we get in the station wagon and drive to Malmesbury. Not for hamburgers or jazz; for an hour Father and Mother can be with Erik. Ian and I sit in the hallway, every now and then we look through the glass, Mother holds Erik on her lap, he laughs open-mouthed with every nurse who walks past, he couldn't care less about being sick.

Afterwards we drive home in silence, the station wagon is hot inside and it feels like hours. Father turns on the radio, even the news is better than our thoughts. Just after the news Gé Korsten sings his latest hit, 'Liefling'. Mother reaches for the radio, we know she's going to search for another station, but she turns up the volume.

You know I can't exist without you, sings Gé.

Mother cries, her face in her hands.

My child, she sobs.

We are not a lovey-dovey family, with the exception of Mother none of us likes hugs and kisses. (At dinner while we say grace Mother gives us a quick hug, we cannot escape or open our eyes, that's sinning.) Group emotions are forbidden, it is too horrible for words, if one person cries or becomes sentimental, the others immediately disappear, it's so repulsive; we prefer anger or irritation, that's in our blood.

But now we are trapped in Mother's tears, the hot station wagon and Gé's fervour. We want our baby brother. Father bites his lip. I don't make a sound, I look straight ahead and feel the tears running down my neck. Ian sits bolt upright next to me, he looks at Mother, leans sideways and looks at Father, turns his head and looks at me. His bottom lip begins to tremble, he turns red in the face and lowers his head. Slowly he lifts his head again and opens his mouth. A groan escapes his throat, then an unearthly, blood-curdling yell, a primal howl during a sacrifice. He cries with his whole body, loudly and without holding back, it is like a fire chased by a strong wind, round and round the inside of the station wagon. We are powerless, all four of us cry as loudly as possible. Past fields of wheat, past the two rows of trees, into the town, in at our gate and into the garage. There is no dinner, we don't brush our teeth, we don't say goodnight, we get into bed, we are exhausted.

Exodus

: Pleased to meet you. Is it my imagination or have we met? Your face looks familiar.

: Pleased to meet you. No, I don't think we've met.

: Perhaps the conference last year? Or the exhibition? With the farming equipment?

: Definitely not, I work with leather.

: Leather?

: Yes, my place can produce anything from leather. We are known in particular for the straps you use to give children a hiding.

: Straps?

: Yes, it's a nice wide strip of leather with a handle. Very comfortable. Some people prefer a belt or a whip, but those things leave marks and then the children can't wear sports uniforms or swim for a long time, it looks too bad.

: Interesting.

: Yes, with our product you can give a child a proper hiding without it leaving unpleasant welts. And you just hang it behind a door or toss it in a drawer, you can keep a few around the house.

: Does it sell well?

: We can't keep up. Here's my card. Come and have a look someday, you can even bring along the naughty child, then you can give him a test hiding and see which one works the best.

Could such a conversation have taken place in my lifetime? Is it at all possible? Could such words have been exchanged without entire flower species falling ill or small animals becoming extinct? Is that how the sun loses some of its light? I suspect as much. There was such a thing in our home. A sick-brown piece of leather with a handle of thicker leather. It was called The Strap and was kept in the kitchen.

I was never a naughty child. But I was unpredictable. For an ordinary family that only wanted to strive for happiness, obey laws, believe what they were told, fit in and follow along, I was incomprehensible, certainly undeserved. Despite my fear, my hunger and my revulsion, I talked non-stop, tested boundaries, delivered judgements, questioned rules, criticised habits. I could test my mother to breaking point. Without wanting to, I could irritate and provoke my father to the point of desperation.

Ian now slept in the room next to The Five Holes Of The Constant Chord. Erik was in his cot in Father and Mother's room. I moved to the bedroom next to the sitting room. This was a big room with a door to the porch and more light than the rest of the house. Here I was supposed to be happier and get rid of The Heavy Castle. But every day I felt more weight settle on my shoulders, I was bent double by my quarrels with my mother. I didn't want to take piano lessons any more, the grand lady with her grand piano and boiled sweets had cast a dark shroud over my heart, I hated every note, I didn't want to open my books, I no longer drew neat clouds and colourful flowers around the titles of my music pieces, I refused to practise the monotonous melodies. My mother forced me to sit at the piano. I didn't lift a hand. I sat without making a sound until my stomach and my head hurt.

Do you know what this piano cost? Do you know what we pay for a piano lesson? Do you know how hard your father works? my mother kept asking.

Sell it, I said, I don't want it.

It's all you want! my mother answered.

That was true. It was all I thought about, music and food. Music like on the English radio station or when visitors came and held a concert, music like in my head, resounding, majestic chords, not the childish plunking with which the cross old woman tried to kill me. I spat poison, I talked back and said things that a child in a conservative household during a country's darkest years should never say. At night my mother told on me, my father said I had to wait in my room, then he went to fetch The Strap.

It didn't hurt, I never felt any pain. It was the physical position, the bending of the body, the neck being held, the strange view of feet on a brown bedroom carpet, the distorted dance of two beings, one a victim because of his age and size, the other a victim despite his age and size, it was wrong, wrong.

I don't want to do this, my father said.

Then the sound followed, the fall of the blows, just a few, but unmistakably the sound of barbarism, the chaotic noise of generations' stupidity.

Have you ever been beaten? And you? You too? Recently I asked this of everyone my age, everyone I could get hold of. Beaten, thrashed, walloped, flogged, hit, caned, tanned, every person used another term, everyone confirmed it.

Why doesn't anyone talk about it? I asked. Everyone is in therapy or denial or on pills or drunk or stoned or bitter or violent as well! Nobody has ever mentioned it!

Why do we have to harp on it now? It was common then, someone said, It was normal.

Normal. That it's never been. The humiliation was staggering, the harm was massive and permanent.

Father is home! Ian would yell at night and run outside. I stayed in my room. I didn't know the term yet, but my attacker was back in the house. The one who was supposed to make me feel safe filled me with fear. At dinner I was quiet.

Aren't you feeling well? my mother asked.

She was the tattletale, that word I did know.

I don't want to do this. I don't want to do this. How many times did he say that? I heard it, but I knew: here it comes, here my world turns upside down again, here come the carpet and the feet.

One evening it is happening again. First blow, second blow. I remember I have a soldier, a prince, a staircase that has risen, I turn my head and bite my father's thigh. It's a deep bite, a wolf sinks its teeth into soft flesh.

Let go! my father yells.

I hold on.

Let go!

I hold on. There's blood.

He throws down The Strap and lets go of my neck. He storms out of the room. For a few days the house is quiet. It's a new atmosphere. A still, heavy cloud that hangs low, full of thunder and lightning, ominous but silent. It would become a very familiar cloud.

Eventually the household goes back to what it knows. Mother cleans, Ian plays at school, plays at home, loses his temper once a day, the woman from the semi-detached house brings biscuits, I wander around the old-age home, reluctantly practise my stupid piano pieces, Erik crows with joy among his toys, Father goes to work with a plaster on his thigh.

It is a month or two later, again I've said something or criticised Mother's cooking, I don't know, it is early evening and I am brushing my teeth. Ian is very unhappy about something in the dining room, he growls like a bear and balls his fists until his anchovy sandwich begins to bulge between his fingers. Erik is sitting next to the table on his blanket and singing at a supernatural volume while hitting an empty cake tin with a plastic hammer. Father enters through the back door and with vehemence Mother paints my unforgivable offence. She ends with the words, If you don't do it now, I'll do it myself.

Where is The Strap? says Father.

With a mouth full of white foam and toothbrush in hand I am out the front door, through the gate, down the road, round the church, right at the skating rink, up the high street, up the hill, out of town. I'm not out of breath, I don't get tired, there isn't a stitch in my side like at a school race. My mouth feels like powder because of the toothpaste that's begun to dry. But my mind is clear and ordered. No one will ever hit me again, I am special – definitely unbelievably special; I'm not running away from punishment, I am leaving now, hopefully I'll be found by my soldier or rescued by people who understand that I need to be somewhere exceptional, a place where fear doesn't live, where stupid rules are banned, where talented children (the organ teacher has said again and again that I am talented, are you deaf?) aren't attacked. There I will make new music, *my* compositions. Or I perish tonight in the veld, ripped apart by animals, it will be in the newspapers, people will mourn for years and then the laws will change.

My father must have run to the garage, we don't have a bakkie. Just past the avenue of trees (more avenues! more running!) he appears next to me.

Get in, he says.

He looks like someone else, tired and defeated, his eyes are red.

I'm off the road. My father makes a wide turn into the veld. He stops in front of me and lowers his head to the steering wheel. I stand still, suddenly out of breath; heaving, I walk around the bakkie and open the other door. We drive home without a word. In my room I put on my pyjamas, the heavy cloud fills the place.

Cotton Wool

I want to pee, says the sunflower next to me.

You can't pee, or eat, says the tulip on my other side, Your leaves are too wide for the door.

My knees are itching, says the tree behind me, Who is going to scratch them? Mom! My knees!

Your mother is already seated, please don't yell, says the teacher who only wears long skirts. Christina, go and scratch Jacques, but carefully, you're going to knock your spots off.

Christina ignores the order and stands in front of me. She is a red mushroom with big white spots.

I don't like this at all, she says, I walk into everything. I want to be the princess.

I also want to be the princess, I say.

Eww, you can't say that! Boys can't be girls! That's devil talk! says Christina.

It's a concert, I say, You can be what you want. And I don't want to be a girl, I just want to sing something pretty, the princess has all the best songs.

You don't have to sing, says Christina, You can play the piano and the recorder. And my mother says your voice is funny, you don't speak properly, you sound like when the wind blows through our broken window, whistling instead of talking.

I am the king! I say, You don't even have a song!

I turn around, I want to stand somewhere else, but there are so many children, they are flowers, shrubs, gnomes, cats, ballerinas, a sun, a moon, tin soldiers, a cow with a big rip across its back, rocks and tufts of grass. There are children in the dressing rooms on either side of the stage, children in the corridors, children in the side hall, it is a whirlpool of cardboard, crepe paper, ribbons, satin, sequins, cloth shoes with curly toes, pointy hats of felt, headdresses of leaves, long beards of cotton wool, tall wigs of cotton wool, lipstick freckles, paper lashes and raffia braids. The doctor's son is in a cape with little gems. I am transfixed. The pale daughter of the pale woman (who lives husband-less in the town's biggest house and smokes in her long motor car) is in a long golden dress with a train full of golden tassels. My mouth falls open.

I look down. I am in my dressing gown with the red and grey stripes. My mother has sewn cotton wool around the sleeves, the collar and the bottom. On my head is a crown of red cardboard. Mother has glued silver stars around the edge, in front is a row of stars running from the bottom to the highest point. I had to stand still for hours while Mother fashioned a beard and a moustache from cotton wool and tried to stick it to my face. I didn't mind, we'd been rehearsing this concert for months and the day of the performance had finally arrived. I trembled when I thought of my entrance. Could anything more wonderous happen to a person? The beard refused to stay put; at her wit's end, Mother finally washed the glue off my chin, grabbed a black pen and drew a moustache. She had to draw it three times, I sweated like only a fat child could. I didn't complain or nag, I was on a cloud. (This cloud was also made of cotton wool, like the three that were already hanging over the stage.) These were the happiest moments I had ever experienced, it was as though friendly electricity kept tickling me with small shocks. I waited on the porch with my plastic sword; finally the whole family was ready and we walked to the church hall, Ian with a book under his arm, Erik on Father's arm – babies were welcome at school concerts.

The operetta was called *Princess Roselyn*. I never had any idea what it was about. Persuading sixty children that they live in a wood and have to sing and dance as nicely as possible, and then on top of that persuading some of them that they are trees and flowers and aren't allowed to move except perhaps to sway, to create a stage set out of cardboard and powdered paint without anything cracking or peeling, to marshal madness in such a manner that an entire rural community sits still for a full hour, to do all of this without resorting to murder was an insane, impossible affair. But it was done and now everyone waited for the verger to turn off the lights and for Corlea's busybody mother to open the curtain.

I was King Rosekrans, a character I played with less masculinity or authority than half a toffee apple (*everybody* knew I would have been the world's best princess, but try to explain that to an impatient, tired teacher who only wears long skirts and has to drive through from Clanwilliam every day because her husband refuses to move even though you can be medically unfit in any town), I knew it was hopeless, in a school concert children don't have choices, but on this night, amid all the homemade costumes and cheap décor, I didn't care, there was a crown on my head, I was cocooned in cotton wool, I was going to be at the centre of the stage and sing and a hall full of people had to watch until I finished.

There was a moment of silence just before my song had to start. There was a cough and a snort and a giggle. Then I sang. Somewhere in the story someone must have disappeared, I will never forget the words to the song: 'We search and we search, but we still can't find him . . .' (For almost fifty years this song has been running through my mind, an appropriate theme song for many occasions.)

There was no applause, the song had to be interrupted, a palace guard or a gnome had to yell that somebody was on their way, everyone had to stare expectantly at an imaginary path somewhere to the right of the stage, the story had to run its course. I couldn't believe it was over. What kind of life was waiting without glue and paint and sequins and cardboard? How do you ever find happiness again without a waggling mushroom or a stumbling tree? We walked back home, Erik sleeping with his head on Father's shoulder.

Your moustache is still there, said Mother.

I don't know why they hold these things on a weeknight, said Father.

Later, everybody was already asleep, I got out of bed and put on the dressing gown. I stood in front of the mirror and stared for a long time. In the dark the cotton wool looked like fur, I was rich and from far away. The next night I pulled on the dressing gown again, put on the crown and drew a moustache myself. I asked Father to take a picture, I still have it, I am standing next to my bed, my sword in front of me, I'm bravely trying to smile, I could see Father wasn't in the mood.

The next night I put on the dressing gown again and every night after that. Each time another piece of cotton wool fell off. Eventually nothing was left. Then Mother put the dressing gown in the wash.

In my mind is a cupboard, in the cupboard is a drawer, in the drawer is a shining light. Now that the cupboard has been opened and the drawer pulled out, the light shines in an endless bright-white streak. It is a beam from below to above, like a sunrise in a puppet show. The drawer can never close again, the light still shines and will shine for as long as my mind still works.

The House At The Top

The high street ran right through town like a straight trail of slug slime without stopping at either end. At the top, just outside town, the road split in two, straight on to Eendekuil or left to Piketberg. At the bottom the road went to Gouda and split later, left to Tulbagh, right to Wellington. On both sides the end of town was demarcated by an avenue of trees, until the night of the toothpaste less frightening than the one outside Riebeek-Kasteel. (Here the athletics track was in the town!)

In the high street, up on the hill, just before the very last side street, there was a four-way stop. On the one corner on the left-hand side there was tall grass or a building that left no impression, on the opposite corner was the co op, an ugly grey monstrosity full of farm smells and burlap sacks. The front of this greyness had two doors, one big and the other small; the smaller one led to The Corner Of Delights – a title I gave and used in quiet. Here you braved screws, rakes and old men for the sake of a few jars on a counter. Bright apricot sweets (always really crisp and freshly made, no tooth was ever broken), marshmallow fish, Chappies bubble gum in yellow wrappers (these were bought for the stories on the inside, why would you want to chew something that you can't swallow?) and thick Wilson's toffees, on a hot day as soft as fudge.

On the right-hand corner was the house where the Winded Woman lived. She was plump and friendly, but always about to expire. Every day she charged down the hill. Exercise, exercise!

Afternoon!

I can't stop, my heart will give out! Afternoon!

The rest of the time she slaved in a wild vegetable garden that constantly defeated her. And twice a week she got into a big tub and trampled beet leaves. With these she apparently made the tastiest stew imaginable, she was just too winded to invite anyone over.

The Hanekoms lived on the last of the four corners. Their house was on the road, and at first glance you would never guess that behind this facade was the biggest erf in any town on any planet. Their back yard began with a garden and ended with a barn, a sawmill, stacks of wood as high as the pyramids of Egypt and right at the end, a forest.

It is at this corner that Father turns right one day, drives past the Hanekoms and stops.

Look, he says, and points to the left.

Mother and I wind down our windows. Next to the road is a low fence of wooden posts and rails, then a bright-green lawn begins that goes on and on, climbing up the hill. Right at the top is a willow, majestic and round like the head of a giant. A house peeks out from behind the willow, a longish, flat house with an open porch, a simple white building without any of the frilliness that the old houses have to put up with.

It's our new home, says Father, Do you want to have a look?

Ian climbs over me and hangs out the window.

Nobody step on the grass, it's mine! he yells, Only cowboys are allowed on the grass, the Indians live under the tree!

Father reverses a few metres and turns in at an untarred road. Our own road! Slowly he drives up to the house. Just above the roof a few silver clouds glide away from one another, sunbeams form an upside-down fan and a choir sings one major chord: Haaaah! Light falls across the green, across our hearts, across our lives. Deliverance! It is impossible that The Heavy Castle or The Strap or the piano can move uphill into this roomy paradise.

Within a month we are settled. I have a bedroom with modern built-in cupboards, bookshelves and a desk Father built himself. The kitchen is big and light, the window overlooks the neighbours' orchard, there is a long, enclosed porch divided by a fireplace into a dining room and a sunroom, a double door with lots of windows opens onto the front porch. Here there is a whole row of cement pots with kumquat trees. Kumquats! Grandmother's little oranges! I cannot explain this, but even during the most difficult moments of growing up these little trees lifted my suffering soul. Toast with kumquat jam, soft cheese with bottled kumquats, bourbon cake with candied kumquats, these tastes were fixed over the years and now rest, stately and royally, in The Rooms Of Riches.

The willow tree becomes my home. Every day, like a pope in the Sistine Chapel, I lie back and stare at the dome. The strings of leaves dangle to the ground, I discover silence, privacy and greatness, nobody says a word, on my own I get to know the dignity of something that was born long before us and will exist long after us. An old prophet with long arms lives in our yard, he protects and shelters, warns with a soft rustle, comforts with his calm presence.

In The House At The Top our family forms new habits. Every afternoon I am allowed to listen to the radio (after homework!). On Springbok Radio I find a new gateway. I listen to Esmé and Jan, wonder why my mother never tries out their recipes; I leave Porterville and fall deeply into the drama of *Dans van die flamink*, lose my heart to every beautiful voice in *Ongewenste vreemdeling*. I start to write my own stories and fill books with drawings of heroes and heroines.

Mother starts doing crafts. A wave of creativity has hit the town and every second woman has a wooden board and a suitcase full of chisels. Woodcarving is all they live for, feverishly they chop and chisel, alone or in groups. Sunflowers, biblical urns, Ruth and Orpah, Paul Kruger and Moses, lions and horses, lilies and proteas, anything and everything appears in wood. These hang above fireplaces, deface front doors, take pride of place on pulpits and peer from bedside tables. They sand and varnish, mount and unveil, eventually everything in town is made of wood. By the time Ma'am organises a tea party to inaugurate the two-metre-long mermaid on her garage door, people finally start rebelling.

No, nonsense, says the Winded Woman, What is this? Wood hell?

Yes, says Corlea's busybody mother, I now only do macramé, it's lovely on a veranda. And the sweetest presents!

Within two weeks three ferns in macramé holders hang in the corner of the sunroom. My mother knots ropes and strings wooden beads and clay balls. I am also knotting. It's like eating in secret, you want to stop but you can't. My mother's friend from the farm goes to the co-op once a week and then pops over for tea. One day she appears with a basket of freshly laid eggs. The macramé is all over the dining room.

I didn't think it's possible to find anything more repellent than my husband's mind, but here it is, large as life, she says.

That same day Mother is done with macramé. She puts the basket of eggs on the counter and takes two flat roasting tins from the cupboard.

Eric is sleeping, she says, Check that Ian doesn't disappear, I'll be next door. Two minutes.

She comes back with one of Aunt Hanekom's recipes. She cracks a few eggs and separates the yolks from the whites. I haven't seen her bake anything since the train cake. This day she bakes a jam roll, golden, light, no cracks, wonderful. The next day she bakes two, the day after that another two. My mother bakes jam rolls without end, she only rests on Sundays. Sometimes they have cream inside, other times only jam, sometimes caramel, occasionally the whole thing is made of chocolate. Soon we are sweet to the marrow. My father says his stomach feels funny. My mother says it's stress. She bakes more and hands out the cakes in town. This jam-roll phase lasts more than two years, totally inexplicable and never discussed to this day.

In the meantime I'm still knotting macramé. I agree with the farm friend, it's disgusting, but it's something that begins and ends, it's an object, a small achievement. There is no interference, no comment, I make each one differently, each is my own idea. I am still drawing books full of heroes, but it is not enough, I learn how to dip candles in wax, colourful nightmares with points and holes and curls, some are covered in glitter, there is enough bad taste in town to find a home for each one. I start doing French knitting, long many-coloured wool sausages are rolled up into bathmats, tablemats, covers for round cushions and bottoms of dog beds. I am feverish, I start doing string art. Nails are hammered into a formation on a wooden board, from deep to shallow or the other way around, then it gets painted, I like white, then crochet yarn is looped and stretched into pictures in bright colours, yachts, palm trees, sand dunes, Christmas trees and dolphins.

Oh, that's pretty, pants the Winded Woman.

She hangs a swan and a dove in her front room.

At school a teacher hears about my home art. It is decided that I will be excused from class for the last two periods each Tuesday, when I will give handicraft lessons to the support class.

The support class has children of all ages, some are eager, others say out loud they're not interested. Two of the boys look like grown-ups and have to shave. I look at my hands and show them what I can do. I am shy and scared, but my enthusiasm gets the upper hand. They learn slowly, walk around, talk back and eventually start getting it right. Proudly we finish one project after the other, just not string art, the teacher says hammers are too dangerous. I begin looking forward to Tuesdays, it's my first step towards leadership and every week I feel more comfortable, the children make jokes and the other teachers have a look, there's even an exhibition in the school foyer.

One day we have to vacate the class because one of the shaving boys has unzipped his trousers.

Hands over eyes! yells the teacher, Into the hallway! Look through your peephole!

It is close to the end of the year and the teacher decides that for the last few weeks we won't have any crafts. The next year there is a new teacher and she has no need of my abilities. So ends my era of handicrafts. I don't regret this, I am growing fast, my head is buzzing and the homemade horrors have gone out of fashion.

The House At The Top changed us. Here were space, breath, light and almost peace. But the piano still stood in the corner of the sitting room; once a day I dragged my feet to the brown beast, sighed – a sigh was always a striking radio moment and I could sigh with the best of them – and raised the lid. On the days when I couldn't get myself that far, Mother made sure that I did. Now and then the house angel saw paralysis really was weighing down my arms, then the phone would suddenly ring or there would be a knock at the front door.

I knew that music was oxygen, that I couldn't live without it, but in a small town music consisted of piano lessons, nothing else. I didn't know that children across the world were busy with violin classes, singing lessons, youth orchestras, Spanish dancing, tap dancing, ballet, jazz, saxophone or the drums. Here it was only nagging, monotony and exams, morsels of the music I could hear within myself.

A child is a remarkable being, despite innocence and ignorance able to survive even with mountains spinning towards him. And this piano tutoring to which I was chained was only one of the Three Shadows that would soon hang over me.

Shadow Two

Across from us there lived a wealthy woman. She travelled the world with an aristocratic attitude and a double string of pearls. We didn't know if she should be addressed as Aunt or Ma'am or Your Highness, and just nodded nervously when she made a rare appearance. At the end of each trip she stayed in her town house for a month, the month after that on her farm outside town, and then she boarded another ship. Two or three times Mother and I were invited to her big living room. Tea was served in hand-painted porcelain, along with shop biscuits on a crystal platter. The walls were covered in paintings, tapestries, embroidery work and hand-woven cloths from the countries she had visited. Above the fireplace was a drawing, thin, neat ink lines on tightly stretched dark-yellow silk depicting an unusual building, seen from the air. She saw me studying it and explained that it was the home of a Chinese nobleman. They built their enormous houses in a square around a courtyard, verandas faced inward and everything was perfectly symmetrical, it had the air of an exclusive community and was easy to defend against enemies. Immediately I liked our school a little bit better: it was built exactly the same way.

The school was at the edge of town, a big square with all the class-rooms opening onto verandas running around the inner court-yard, a perfect square. In the centre was the hall. The school was surrounded by a rugby field, tennis courts, music rooms, play-grounds, and at the front a rose garden with a sundial. Across the road was the dormitory where farm children and a few teachers stayed.

I was a primary-school pupil and against all expectations a few things did bring me joy, above all, my schoolbooks. We were allowed to cover our books – textbooks and exercise books – in any paper we liked. All the books were new, nothing was handed down or used for a second year. New books with patterned paper and shiny cellophane, it was like Christmas! In every shop I searched for sheets of wrapping paper, rolls of paper were dragged into the house, no two books looked the same, stripes for language, leaves for geography, curls for composition, squares for sums; for a few moments I was crazed with happiness. Each book was carefully placed, each sheet of paper was marked, lines were drawn, outlines were cut as though life itself would end with the slightest error. Perfectly covered, name written in front, cellophane wrapped and taped to make sharp corners, each book placed upright in my new schoolbag of soft leather. I couldn't wait to take out a book in class so a teacher would stare or a jealous girl look in annoyance at her own brown paper. Most earthly crea-tures will never experience or understand this: to handle, read and then display an attractive, cared-for book remains a privilege, an exceptionally elegant experience; the smell of a new book re-mains a confirmation of progress and hope.

Break at school was a foretaste of all the misery and violence of which humanity was capable; survival was an art form that had to be learnt at speed and exercised with purpose. As early as the fifteenth century, Hieronymus Bosch depicted a playground as a hell full of vicious primitives. For those never-ending twenty minutes I wandered and bounced about on this dusty flatness, a baby rat on a drifting raft. There were gangs, they eyed each other, hid, defected and formed new gangs. Why? I wondered. Kill each other or let it go, just make a decision! Little boys dug holes until the earth's crust looked like nothing would ever rid it of the plague. Around each hole a group knelt and shot marbles, an indecipherable game. I also arrived with my bag of marbles, glass balls with lovely coloured flecks inside, I knelt, shot repeatedly, each time hit something the wrong way and was chased away. At home I emptied my bag into a glass bowl and put it in front of my bedside light, the patterns danced against walls, messengers from an impossibly distant kingdom.

Bigger children lurked like predators, always looking to draw blood, cretins with coarse faces and bodies stuck in that painful phase before good proportions could create comfort or good looks. They looked for trouble, taunted, pushed, tripped, stole, pinched, grabbed; I was a perfect target, soft face, soft body, soft voice, a piglet among hyenas. I fled and ducked, wished, prayed and hid. Begone. Don't look. Leave me alone. I am only visible in class. Away with your sweaty paws. Away with your hot breath. I am here to achieve. I'm not your friend.

There were friends. Four. The neighbours' youngest son. The postmaster's son. The friendly teacher's son. And the lonely woman's son. They could see me. They did not condemn or wound. They could play rough, but also read, and talk for hours.

They were curious and adventurous. Weekends we had sleepovers. At one boy's home we stayed up at night and stole skuinskoek from a tin taped shut with sticking plasters: the skuinskoek was a precious treat, baked and sent by a grandmother in Sutherland. At another's home we had to go to bed early, we had to be inside our dreams before his mother and father finished the wine and began arguing loudly. At yet another's home, drawings from the *Huisgenoot*'s love stories were studied by flashlight and then we practised kissing, open mouthed with long tongues and lots of spit, it was horribly disgusting and absolutely delicious. Sis, we whispered, Again!

A lunchbox was something that had to wait in your bag until you wanted to faint from hunger, until you forgot for a moment that break was deathly and began praying for the bell to ring. A lunchbox was like an old person, there were good days and bad days. On a good day there was white bread with tomato and cheese or a roll with ham and mayonnaise. Even a Chomp or a Kit-Kat. On a bad day there was brown bread with Marmite or, devastation of devastations, apricot jam. I begged my mother for tuck money, I pleaded with my father, I lied and said children stole my sandwiches, I said I threw up because the heat made the sandwiches taste off, I offered to work for money. Eventually I got tuck money, once or twice a week; on other days I first tried the lunchbox and then begged some vetkoek or Provitas off one of my four friends. Days with tuck money were like holidays. I wasn't anxious or on the lookout for cretins, I rushed to the tuck-shop counter next to the hall and wrestled my way to the front. Here two dormitory matrons supplemented their pensions by selling hot dogs and packets of chips. With a steaming miracle in one hand and a packet of salt-and-vinegar in the other I slipped into the hall and ate behind the choir stalls. This feast made all the suffering, every single terrifying schoolday, worth the trouble. Years later I relived this pleasure as a student at Stellenbosch every time I slipped into the church and ate a hot dog behind the organ.

It is a Monday, all of us are seated in the hall, the principal has made his last announcement, it is time for the school anthem. Every evil spirit with a free hand grabs a shadow and drags it to right above my chair and my faith. A man with an acorn head and a red skin, dressed in a blue nylon tracksuit with white stripes, walks up to the podium and announces that summer is almost over, this winter every boy will play rugby, if anyone doesn't know what the correct rugby uniform is, find out, we are practising according to age groups, the roster appears at break on every notice-board.

For two days I have no idea what's happening around me, all sounds turn into thunder, I protest, ask questions, explain that I am ill, nobody hears my voice, nobody sees my panic, Father laughs about the rugby playing, his voice is thunder, Mother complains about the price of sportswear, her voice also thunder. Wednesday I am standing on the field, white shorts, wine-red jersey with a mustard-yellow stripe, it is our first practice session, other boys jump about impatiently, yell and tackle each other, they can't wait for the action to start. The man in the blue tracksuit appears and blows his whistle. Everything on earth, everything that has ever been familiar or merciful, comes to a halt. Like oil stains on a puddle of water we move soundlessly, without purpose or direction. We assume positions, the tracksuit yells and roars, slaps my shoulder, pulls my arm, I end up in a line, I end up in a huddle, I end up on my knees. My face is wet.

Am I crying? Boys laugh. Later they look surprised. Am I being picked on? I don't know anything.

We are on a bus. We end up in a strange town, there are groups of people around a sports field, also Father and Mother and Ian and Erik. Strange boys in other colours charge at us. We run, we fall. I scurry like an animal that's been fed poison. The tracksuit yells at me. Thunder. I remember Grandfather talking of a pig in socks. Was that him?

I look up, the ball drops from the sky like a dead dove. It's in my arms. What should I do? A child as big as a horse charges at me. I remember my shorts are white, I remember how upset Mother gets when she has to wash white things a second time. I throw the ball at the horse child. People scream like madmen. The child catches the ball and storms past me. My shorts are still white. Why is everyone yelling?

The next day is a Sunday. After church my friend waits for me in front of the church.

The whole town is talking about you, he says, Because you passed the ball to the enemy.

I didn't know I shouldn't, I say.

You pass it to your own team, he says, Or you run to the goalposts.

Then why do they give us white shorts? I ask.

You shouldn't go to Sunday school, he says, They'll get you.

I sit behind the parsonage until Sunday school is finished. I only walk home once the streets are quiet. I am nauseous. I am nauseous the whole week, I don't even buy a hot dog or a packet of salt-and-vinegar. The next Saturday we play rugby in Darling. There are so many people that some have to stand on the backs of bakkies to see anything. Everybody has heard about me. And that our team is going to lose by the biggest margin in history. We do not disappoint.

This hell lasts for months. During practice the tracksuit hits me with a thin plank, the kind the Hanekoms make fruit crates out of. We are learning how to scrum.

Break! he screams.

I am too slow and get two blows to the thigh.

I curse him without making a sound. I know you shouldn't curse someone, but I do curse him, again and again, I curse him with every misfortune I can think of.

Now, here on paper, it sounds melodramatic, but it is still part of my body, the knowledge of betrayal, the evil of peer pressure, the gall of mass pleasure, the hopelessness of fighting against rubbish like running around and getting hurt on a lawn just because thousands, thousands, thousands worship it.

Nowadays it is hilarious, my escapades on a rugby field, but as a child of eleven I experienced it as hate. Hate for me and therefore my hate for them, the organised, thick-skinned, short-sighted, traditional, legal, public bullies. This was where my deep-seated aversion to authority of any kind began, my dislike of politicians, academics, churchly kings and social giants. My resistance to bending or following still leads to closed doors.

Seven months after I passed the ball to the enemy, the tracksuit's wife left him and his child failed his year. I asked Grandfather and Grandmother to take me to Paarl; there I could buy stars and glitter for the new year's schoolbooks.

Pontiac

Summer finally arrives. For the first time in my life heat brings relief. We still have to participate in sports, but now there is a choice between athletics and tennis. Most children choose athletics, run and jump and throw and yell, that's where their love lies.

Only a few of us play tennis. The courts are behind the school, next to the untarred road and across from a big field. We are surrounded by a high dark-green hedge, our instructor is Mrs Louw, the mother of one of my four friends, she chooses the quietest afternoon of the week, I almost feel safe.

We learn to serve, follow through with the forehand, build strength with the backhand, play at the net, play away from the net. We have white shoes, white shirts, sometimes white caps (I look like an egg that's been peeled from the bottom and avoid the cap) and brand-new rackets. My racket has a white leather cover with a red zip – as usual the packaging makes me the happiest. Tennis is a type of sport, a physical activity, thus I am hopeless and lose every possible point, but there are only eight of us, four boys and four girls, so I make the team. Now I can be humiliated in every town in the Swartland, yippee.

Before my first tournament someone whispers in my ear, it's not The Prince, it's a woman's voice, high and breathy, perhaps Bora, perhaps Becca.

You have to have confidence, the voice says, Hit high.

I have no idea what that means. Our very first tournament is in Moorreesburg. The boys go with Mr Olivier, his son is also on the team. Mr Olivier is one of the teachers who teach the bigger children, he is an older man, friendly and always in a tailor-made suit that fits perfectly. They live at the end of our street, a corner erf with the house surrounded on all sides by a neat garden.

Mr Olivier lives with two things that many envy him, a very old car and a very young wife. This wife is beautiful with hair like Jackie Kennedy and make-up like Sophia Loren. Before we leave we drink cooldrink. I stare, how can she be anyone's mother? Where do you find a dress like that? Soft fabric with an autumn leaf motif, draped round the waist and hips like she's going to dance in one of Fred Astaire's musicals.

On this earth there are buildings or objects that can transport you with only a touch or a glance. One such thing is parked in front of the garage, a dark-grey Pontiac. Mr Olivier and his son get in the front, the rest of the team in the back. Inside it is as big as a rich man's bar, one of those where city people smoke cigars, hold etched tumblers and clinch deals that no government can ever know of. Seats of antique leather with fine cracks, chrome handles on the doors, polished wooden panels, a pull-out tray for drinks, small drawers for sweets or coins, a radio that can surely receive Russian codes.

Mr Olivier laughs more than once and says, I dream of a new car, but your father does such good work that this old wagon just keeps on running!

The early seventies gave birth to the most disturbing fashions, furniture and architecture in history, shapes, textures and colours, nowadays collected by eccentrics, may they never be repeated. In this Pontiac, completely out of place while it slowly drifts through the wheat fields on our way to Moorreesburg, I sit back like a proper lord in a European novel, without a worry in the world, blind to the jealousies and squabbles among his workers or tenants. The little jackals that gnaw at the heels of mere mortals have never been inside a Pontiac.

We stop at the tennis courts in Moorreesburg. Immediately I forget about my spectacular arrival: the boy against whom I have to play has legs like a leopard, I want to draw him next to the other heroes in my book, not play against him. I feel how my body turns to stone and melts again. I am a fat baby and I want my bottle.

The leopard has first serve. He tosses the ball in the air and hits it so hard I can hear the court crack.

Hit high, says the voice.

I lower my racket and swing it backwards like a lady who wants to knock down an attacker with her groceries. With a straight arm I jerk the racket to the front, the ball flies into the air, higher and higher. The other children shade their eyes with their hands and crane their necks backwards.

Where is the ball? yells my friend.

The child's serving soup! yells Moorreesburg's instructor.

The leopard tripples to and fro. He holds his racket in both hands. Like a comet the ball shoots back to earth. The leopard swipes wildly at the air. The ball hits the court.

It's in! yells my friend.

That's not tennis! yells Moorreesburg's instructor.

It's *his* tennis, Mr Olivier says calmly. Always his own ideas, an exceptional pupil.

Again and again the leopard hits. Again and again I send the ball into the heavens. I win the first of many matches. Moorreesburg threatens to lay a charge. Mr Olivier politely takes his leave and we get into the Pontiac. Slowly we drive back, classical and graceful. We drink Cream Soda and eat NikNaks. I forget that I've ever been unhappy.

Airplane, Water, Ivy

In July 2015 I was busy with preparations for MANNEQUIN, my sixteenth stage production for Emperors Palace. As a solo artist it was a major achievement to have had such a long and successful residency at such a big theatre, but every year the stress became more unbearable. So many weeks! Will I fill the theatre? Will everyone come again? How many people are excited and how many are just sharpening their knives? Am I thin enough? Is the music too strange? Is the story gripping? Am I repeating myself?

At night I began to dream, every night the same story. I am at an airport with a group of musicians, the previous night we had a performance somewhere, we are on our way home. A loud voice announces that our airplane is grounded for technical reasons and that we have to go to another terminal to wait for our new flight. One of the musicians remarks that the announcement had been made in an odd accent. Moments later another announcement follows, a plane does not have permission to take off, those passengers also have to go to the other terminal. Other, similar announcements follow, hundreds of passengers are streaming in the same direction as us.

The new terminal looks completely different from the rest of the airport, there are no noticeboards, no colourful ads, no restaurants, no shops; it's a massive metal construction with concrete walls and a corrugated-iron roof, no windows. People are anxious about their luggage and look for staff or counters, but there aren't any. A further announcement – now clearly in a very strange accent – is made. Everyone is on the same flight, there are no booked seats, everyone has to board through the doors at the end of the hall.

How is that possible? people yell.

Move! the voice booms over the loudspeakers.

I look for the musicians, they have disappeared, hundreds of people push against one another, some stumble and fall, I don't recognise anyone, I don't want to get on the airplane but the stream is too strong, onwards, onwards. People cry and search for family members or other travel companions.

In the plane I panic. Something is very wrong. There are rows of seats as far as the eye can see, not just in front of me but also to the sides. No airplane is shaped like this, how can a stadium take off?

It's the General Flight, says a woman behind me. Her voice is hoarse with fear.

Don't sit, says a man, They can't take off as long as we remain standing.

I know about the General Flight, says the woman, You disappear. Nobody looks for you, you're just gone.

She grabs my shoulder, The place they're taking you, nobody will see you, you are simply invisible. I've heard that a few found their way back, but nobody recognised them!

I shove people, I lose my bag, I storm past the seats, down the aisle, I don't see one familiar face, I yell everyone's names but my people are gone. Finally I am at the last row, I see the number on the floor, 333. In front of me is a woman in a light-grey uniform. She doesn't have any eyebrows. Her hair is slicked back and fastened in a round thing on top of her head. Behind her is an open door.

No! she says in an unfamiliar language. But you always recognise a no, even when you're busy running into a woman in a uniform. She falls backwards, I tumble over her, out the door. My fall lasts long enough for me to wonder why I'm not waking up, other dreams are usually shorter. Soundlessly I land on soft grass. I jump up and I run, I know where to go, to my left is a long, flattish building of dark wood, the horizontal boards overlap like roof tiles, there is a row of windows, in front of each one a rose bush has been planted, it looks like a train that got stuck in a garden. To my right is an old-fashioned building, two or three storeys high, in front of me is a swimming pool with a white cement edge that rises up from the lawn like a kraal wall on a ghost farm; behind the swimming pool is a square house with a pitched roof and windows neatly arranged one below the other, a big doll's house, completely covered in ivy. That's where I'm going. There are three steps to the front door. A light tap makes the door fly open. I charge inside. The house is empty, no people, no furniture, every wall is covered in wallpaper that looks like wall. I have time to think about this. Were the walls ugly? Who knew that you could cover an ugly wall with a pretty wall?

Inside the ivy house there was peace, I could catch my breath and start to relax. Nobody, not terrorists, murderers, teachers, family or neighbours could find you here. This reassurance was given the moment you pushed open the door. By whom? There wasn't a voice, just the knowledge. Each time I woke up at this moment, exhausted after the General Flight had dragged me away from another night's rest.

The ivy-covered house did exist in reality. It stood on a lawn in the middle of the Hugenote Kollege's other campus, as did the long wooden train, the old-fashioned building and the swimming pool. After Grandmother and Grandfather left House Samuel, they moved here, to a little house right at the edge of the grounds.

I would never have believed there was a more beautiful building on earth than House Samuel, but it was so. If I hadn't started running in my dreams the moment I fell out of the airplane but first looked over my shoulder, I would have seen this castle. Its name was Cummings.

This giant was designed by an American architect and built at the end of the nineteenth century, a mysterious French castle of stone in a town in the Boland. During holidays Grandfather and his team of helpers had to ease the pain of this ghostly, groaning beauty, and I wandered down hallways and through rooms and towers. How many of the stories with which I earn a living today were handed to me here, from behind carved bedroom doors and deserted storerooms! This is where impatience – often revulsion – with the ordinary first settled in my bones.

On Cummings's miniature porch I sat and looked at the old-fashioned building; it was called Ferguson. I never went inside, Ferguson was like an old-school butler, formal and closed up. Officially closed, Grandfather said when I asked. We did go into the cellar quite often. Here Grandfather stored the tools. (Nobody ever said it was a cellar, but that's what it felt like to me, a special floor, lower than the lawn outside, only accessible through a back door or a side door.) Rooms with sandy floors and many spider-webs made it feel as though we were underground. Windows, very low outside, very high inside, sent in rays of light in which dust motes floated around. I could have stared at this for hours, but sneezing fits had me fleeing back outside or to the next room. Here abandoned tables and chairs stood as though a war had interrupted a lesson. Piles of books had been left everywhere, some filled partway with a curly handwriting in fountain pen, paragraphs of which I understood nothing, others bound with thick thread and clad in leather, here and there a gilded name on one of the corners, articles from newspapers, pictures from magazines, carefully pasted in and neatly framed in ink. Here and there were captions, each in a neat handwriting. Why had no one ever fetched these? Didn't anyone need these books? I could name each of my books, title and author, and where each stood on which shelf! What must have happened to make people just abandon their work and ideas like this?

In my textbooks history consisted of Jan van Riebeeck's unwelcome arrival, Blood River and a big to-do with the English, a khaki affair – romanticised in order to wring lifelong loyalty from pupils – which I found so off-putting that today I spend every free moment travelling the world, discovering for myself the lost story of immortal literature, art and music, the cruelty of the mighty church and the bloodthirsty nobles, also the beauty of the mighty church and the bloodthirsty nobles, the unimaginable sacrifice and poverty that made people dedicate their lives, generation after generation, to the erection of a single palace or cathedral to which we flock in our millions today. How different my life might have been if I could have sat in a class in Ferguson's cellar with a fountain pen and a leather-bound book, my name in front in golden letters, while someone told me the truth about the subject that is now my greatest passion?

The swimming pool. Here we spent time on hot days with the family (I now had two little brothers, Magdel had a sister and a brother, every now and then more cousins joined us, there were a lot of us!) on towels and beneath umbrellas. Down the road, behind the tiny little house, Grandmother put chicken thighs, mealies, sausages and tomato-and-onion sandwiches on the coals, then the food was brought over in big metal bowls. I couldn't swim (there had been many attempts, also formal swimming lessons, no success) and I couldn't stand direct sunlight, but I was mad about the inflatable mattresses on the water, the wings on my arms, the plastic duck round my middle, my red sunglasses and the umbrella with the clouds. Somewhere these things were designed by very modern people: they were made of plastic in shockingly bright colours, printed in wild patterns, filled with stars, and no chlorine on earth could chase away the smell of newness. It was like building a stage set, there was enough visual delight to make this extremely physical activity bearable. Until the day Father finally lost his patience and threw me into the swimming pool without my blow-up things. That was how he had taught himself to swim in a farm dam long ago. I didn't even try to swim, I thanked the Lord for everything and studied the cracks in the swimming pool's light-blue floor. Everyone screamed, underwater it sounded like an angelic choir, for a moment I wondered why I couldn't hear a harp, then Father fished me out.

That was my last visit to the swimming pool. But water still remained. Grandmother's tiny little house was right next to a river, the same one that flowed through Donkiebos. The same clear water, the same smooth stones, the same dancing specks of light, the same ancient trees lifting their rheumatic arms into a green roof over the river. Here my cousins and I – the girls, the boys never wanted to join in – enacted rituals, acted out tragedies, balanced on big stones and, dressed in white sheets, tried to awaken the tree spirits. For hours and hours we were soothed by this calm stream, also at night when the water murmured below the open bedroom window.

I did see the swimming pool during every stay, short or long; as many times as possible I went there on my own to look at the ivy-covered house. Like all the other buildings on the campus it was empty during holidays. I never went inside, it wasn't necessary, I sat on the grass, awestruck. The fact that grown-ups, adults – the same ones who were always nagging, pestering, commenting, making rules, knowing better – allowed the ivy to grow and cover every millimetre of this house until only the windows were still visible, that something that was unpractical and useless, something that attracted spiders and could block a drain, was left untouched just so that it could please the eye, boggled the mind. Here it was in front of me: a history I wanted to know.

One day I will die in the house where I now sit and type. It took me seventeen years to make it disappear under the ivy. Nobody can see it. Some think they can, but they're scared and leave us alone. I can never move house, too little time is left to make something like this happen again.

Shadow One, Again

First break ended a minute ago. We stand in line in front of the school's side entrance and wait for the announcements. The child in front of me jerks his head to the right.

What's that? he asks.

All of us jerk our heads to the right. On the other side of the playground is a narrow path, tarred and edged with two thin rows of face brick. This path leads to a smallish building with two music rooms. A figure is moving along this path. It's a woman. Bolt upright as though she's been screwed to scaffolding. A long, open rust-brown cardigan hangs to just below her knees. A long rust-brown blouse with a man's collar hangs to just above her knees. A long rust-brown skirt hangs to just above her ankles. These skirts usually had elastic around the waist and lots of fabric gathered to form pleats that would kick out when you walked. Because of the long cardigan and the long blouse the skirt does not kick out now, it hangs, heavy and uncomfortable, as though items have been sewn into the seams, items that had to be smuggled across a border in a long-past war. The figure ends in white socks and oxblood lace-up shoes with low heels. In the hand closest to us is a walking stick. The walking stick and the leg on the far side hit the ground at the same time, then the whole body lifts up and the leg in the middle kicks forward. When this leg lowers, the whole body lowers. We stand as though hypnotised. Something out of a cartoon has come to entertain us.

It's the new music teacher, says Christina.

Immediately my hypnosis vanishes. Streets away, eager hands grab The Shadow above my piano and pull it, no, stretch it to above the music room. I flee into the school building.

At second break, every child has a stick. Everyone practises the walk, leg and stick down, body up, leg lowers, body lowers, it's not easy. A few get it right, a few applaud and that afternoon everyone has to stay after school for detention.

By that stage I had already gone through a multitude of music teachers, private ladies up and down town, young teachers at school, probationary teachers, substitute teachers, some civilised, some strict, some more afraid than I was, others without any insight or talent.

No one could explain how Miss De Rotterd had ended up at our school. She was from another country.

Fell from a dragon, was Jacques's explanation after the first singing lesson.

And fell hard, said the tall child who could inhale smoke, That's why the leg and the lips don't work.

Miss De Rotterd was originally from Holland, I will never know how long she had wandered and for how long she had been lost before she found us. She was a tall woman, dressed every day in another long shirt, long cardigan and long skirt, all in exactly the same colour, old-green, old-blue, old-red or old-yellow. A grim, blocky cylinder of wool and fibre. She never made eye contact, even if she had to spend thirty minutes teaching thirty children to sing, she could look past everyone. Her small eyes closed, opened, wandered, but never looked into any other eyes. As though bewitched, all of us started doing the same thing, avoiding eye contact with her. To this day, not a single victim can describe her hair, a grey vagueness nesting somewhere above her eyes. The lips no one could miss. Thin lips that moved precisely up and down like the world's first robot, two wishbones from the carcass of a pie chicken, covered in the same chicken's skin. The skin wrinkled and folded when she talked.

It's called muttering, said Joy.

Nobody could hear her. Her voice was too soft and the Dutch accent incomprehensible. We tried reading lips but couldn't make out anything, there were only the robotic movements, slightly up and slightly down.

Attention, attention! she whispered furiously. Then everybody made as much noise as they could. After school we had to report for detention.

Miss De Rotterd was our jailer. Everywhere she went she caused confusion, she got furious and somebody got detention. Sundays the church was full, everybody knew things were going to go pear-shaped, nobody wanted to miss it. She was the new organist and had her own ideas about tempo, preludes and interludes. She constantly launched into the wrong hymn, we stared at our hymn books and tried to figure out what she was doing, then she would suddenly stop playing, turn around, clap her hands and mutter with the wishbones, Again, again! Children ducked below the pews with laughter. The minister sighed and said, Thank you. Please be seated.

My first music lesson was like when a prisoner meets the leader of a new planet. Miss De Rotterd sat to the right of the piano, upright on a wooden chair, the walking stick resting against the windowsill. There was no glance of acknowledgement, no greeting.

Sit, child. Show me what you're busy with.

I sit in front of the piano. My hands tremble. I open the book. Unisa Grade Two. The piece begins with four notes, three with the right hand, one with the left. I play the chord.

Stop!

Her left hand moves to the piano, index finger pointed, thumb and middle finger bent into a circle, the hand is now a revolver. The revolver presses against my wrist until I lift it.

Again!

Chord.

Stop!

Again the revolver comes. Again my position is wrong. My posture is wrong. The strength must come from the shoulder, the wrist must be stiff, rock hard, you don't play with a fly swat, your fingers do the work. From your shoulder to the piano's hammer is one strong mechanism, there are no loose or weak parts in the middle.

Again!

Chord.

Stop!

Revolver.

Finally the bell rings. There was too little time, I have to stay after school for music theory.

Who taught you? You've been robbed of all technique!

No goodbye, the revolver points at the door.

Run *now*, I tell the girl waiting outside. Two weeks later she quits.

I can't quit anything. Our circumstances have changed suddenly, and changed completely. Father has decided he wants to become a minister, maybe only on the radio, maybe only with books, that is his dream, theology. He has gone to study at Stellenbosch, he's away during the week, he stays in Stellenbosch, sometimes in Wellington with Grandmother. He only comes home at weekends, at night he stares with droopy eyes at heavy books, Greek and Hebrew, Mother stays up to help and encourage.

Whatever the plan was, if anything, within months we are penniless. We scrape the bottom of every object and surface to survive. Poverty comes knocking like family who've lost their house. Mother makes plans, she is alone with us five days a week, she has to start working. She was a teacher before I was born and starts to help out at a crèche on a farm close to town. Sally helps in the house and looks after Erik while we're at school. Nothing stays a secret in a town this size: people begin to contribute, baskets of vegetables, rusks and bags of fruit are brought over as though they're all old friends. I am mortified, but there's no time to agonise over anything, Father has a dream and I have a shadow.

Miss De Rotterd was on my case as though she'd been given a mission, nobody could save me, there was theory in the afternoon, practice until the sun went down, piano lessons with the revolver twice a week. She decided I wasn't suffering enough and arranged for me to take the piano exam in Piketberg. I couldn't hide or quit, piano lessons cost money and I knew the whole family were making sacrifices to help me. I knew it didn't have anything to do with my plans, but it was my only link to The Something. The Something had no shape or feature, there was no description, it was the way in which I would function someday, it was The Something that made sure that I was now busy with something that no other boy in town could or would do, The Something was mine, it was the sound I would one day create, the way I would look, the unknown image or shape that waited for me to chisel it out of the chosen stone and give it life. The Dutch robot had me on a leash, there was no escape, when the wishbones talked I obeyed.

Sundays I played my own music, sat at the piano and tried to create order from that which flowed freely through my mind when no one else was around. I played without fear, made rhythms and patterns, I used all the keys from lowest to highest, I used the pedals and opened the top.

Stop that ghlar-ghlar! Mother yelled from the kitchen. (It was her own phrase, that's what my playing sounded like to her. She tolerated my exam pieces, but I'd never know if she enjoyed them. She did ask me to play something when someone came over for tea, not that anyone listened to more than the first few bars.)

Much later I realised that to her the piano held the possibility of achievement, a means to an end, a secure position and a secure income, something for which she yearned now that we (penniless) had to keep on believing Father's studies would lead to an easier life.

It is Sunday again. I play a dramatic chord, something that could make a curtain lift and a figure in a cloak covered in gems – much more expensive than that of the doctor's son – appear in a spot-light. A chord like that could make a thousand people catch their breath, make them jump to their feet and applaud with tears streaming down their cheeks.

It's the day of the Lord! yells Mother, Play a Hallelujah or nothing! What about 'I Walk in the Garden Alone'? That's appropriate!

I go and lie down beneath the willow. The Shadow can't reach in here. I am never leaving here again. Until Mother calls us in for dinner.

Father stays a day longer so he can take me to Piketberg for the exam. I am so scared I can't speak, I can't say a word. He tells me how difficult it is for him to master all his subjects, how much respect he now has for people who persevere, they are the ones who are rewarded. He says it doesn't matter how smart or stupid someone is, or if they have any talent, if they work hard enough they will rise above their circumstances. He says we are humble people from a humble background, but there is no reason for us to stay beggars, we don't have to spend our lives saying yes, sir, thank you, sir. Nobody has been given life just so that someone can breathe down their neck every day. I just nod.

In Piketberg we stop in front of a school. The hill is so steep I am convinced the car is going to run backwards. We get out.

Shouldn't we put rocks behind the wheels? I ask.

Father laughs.

I fixed it myself, it's not going anywhere.

We walk through the gate. The music rooms are just a few steps to the left. In front of a dark-brown door a woman sits behind a table with a bowl of sweet peas and a pile of forms. She gives a friendly hello and says we can sit down and relax, it's still a few minutes before I can go in. She says down the corridor there's another classroom with a piano, do I want to practise a bit? I shake my head. My whole body is weak, I am too unwell to do anything, any moment now I will dissolve, disintegrate, I'll just wait, what does it matter from which piano they have to scrape my remains?

Father and the woman chat away happily.

Oops! says the woman, I'm laughing too much, what if they hear me!

The dark-brown door opens and a tall schoolgirl with a confident smile walks past us.

Your parents are having tea across the road, says the friendly woman, I hope it went well.

No mistakes, says the girl and disappears.

The woman gets up and peers into the room. She nods.

You can go in, she tells me.

A propeller with red and blue stripes sprouts from her head and starts rotating, faster and faster until there is a big purple circle. I can't feel my legs. My father holds out a hairy claw to help me, he has two hairy ears on top of his head, pitch-black whiskers and a long tail. The tail flicks from side to side. He picks me up and throws me into the room. The door slams shut.

I lift my head and look for my book.

You don't need a book here, says a warm, pleasant voice.

I get up. In front of me is a black, upright piano. Next to me is a desk behind which a woman with a wild bush of light-yellow hair is standing. She holds out her hand and grabs mine.

I came all the way from Cape Town, she says, Just to hear you. Relax, fear causes doubt and mistakes, suddenly you see things that aren't there and forget things you've known for ages. I'm sure you know your story, but your eyes look like those of a little mouse. Just before the eagle closes its beak.

I am speechless.

Haahaahaa! she laughs, My name is Helena. I don't eat mice or children. Take a deep breath and then you can sit down. I think we'll leave the scales for later. First we'll listen to your pieces. Which one is your favourite? If you don't have one I forgive you, nobody knows who picks these things! Haahaahaa!

The waltz, I say. I can't believe I have a voice.

Play it, says Helena, Transport me!

I play the waltz. Then the next piece, then another one. I play my scales without a single mistake. I answer all the questions in my wind-through-a-broken-window voice. I even make a joke. It's the first time I've been with a friendly person and an upright piano in the same room.

Haahaahaa! laughs Helena, I hope I see you next year!

The car is still there when we get outside. We walk across the road to a small restaurant. The confident girl is at a table with her parents. Father buys us each an ice cream, white balls in gnomes' hats. We drive back to Porterville. I don't talk this time either, but this silence comes from a happier heart. In front of the black piano there was a moment when I thought I knew what The Something looked like.

Three weeks later I drag my feet to the music room. All the children have already gone home, a few boys are being rowdy on the rugby field, now I have to listen for an hour while the wishbones tell me how tiring it is to look at my poor efforts at music theory.

The robot doesn't greet me. On the table is a long envelope. She taps it with the revolver.

Take it to your parents, she says.

The revolver points at the door.

At home I wait until after dinner, Bible study and the evening story.

Miss De Rotterd sent this, I say and put the envelope on the kitchen table.

Mother opens it and reads for a long time, from top to bottom, every word. It's the piano exam results. I got full marks. The only candidate that year. Helena writes that I am gifted. Mother wipes the tears from her eyes.

You see, she says.

Shadow Three

My bedroom was completely dead; no matter how hard I tried, it had no past, no names, no voices. Somebody must surely have stayed there? Had it been a storeroom before? I began to spend my time in other places, corners and spots where there was less loneliness. Although I preferred being by myself most of the time, I had to feel like I was close to a story, whether past or future made no difference; the most deserted place could be a living space and there I felt better.

This awareness of events, lingering emotions, joys that still lived between the walls, shock or sorrow that hid behind paintings, affected me more and more; sometimes I was moody, other times unnecessarily anxious, occasionally deeply disappointed after days of inexplicable suspense. Only as an independent adult did I realise how severe this condition was. I had to move from flat to flat to find out it was the proximity of others that made me more tired by the day; conflict, emotional violence, jealousy and suspicion seeped through the walls and clamoured for my attention. I had to live in big houses with big yards before I could afford it; to this day I am exhausted after a week in a hotel or a few days in a holiday apartment.

In primary school I couldn't put it into words, I'll try now: being on your own is lovely and necessary, to me it is vital, but at the same time there has to be a presence nearby. It isn't always immediately clear whether this presence attracts or repels me, it takes time to find out.

So I spent more and more time on my little bicycle. I have no idea why I can't just call it a bicycle, maybe I was too fat or too busy growing, in my memories it is always a little bicycle. I cycled through the entire town, some weeks every day, otherwise as much as possible. There wasn't a street I wanted to avoid, everywhere there was the lure of intrigue, almost tangible secrets, fortunes lost in outrageous manners, a long sickbed, a difficult birth, a secret love or an outcast soul. I cycled slowly past these places, sometimes stopped and stared. At familiar ones I knocked on the door and then stayed for hours, the older the inhabitants the better the visit, without thinking they would put a chore aside and welcome you warmly. In between were the dead spaces, inhabited or not; some of these could awaken as incubators of evil, but that happened at night when the streets were empty.

Across from the school was a house on a corner. We visited there one Saturday evening, I remember the woman asking why I was so quiet and my mother explaining that I'd been given a hiding the night before.

I could hear him begging from down the hallway, my mother said, No, Dad, please, Dad, don't, Dad!

If they don't want to learn they have to feel, said the woman.

It felt like I'd cracked open the shame like a pomegranate and smeared it over my face. That house became a dead space. Nothing, nothing, keep going. Down the road towards the showground, then slowly past Uncle and Aunt Wikkie's home. Their house was set towards the front of a big yard with plum trees. Stony ground, small back porch, a kitchen filled with milk tarts under gauze domes, the best milk tarts ever. Nobody could reproduce the recipe. There were stories of a woman in Velddrif who swirled brandy in her mouth and then spat it into the batter. Maybe that was Aunt Wikkie's secret. Aargh, sis! was the reaction, but the orders still streamed in.

In the side street was the new parsonage with the handsome minister. He turned up without a wife, unheard of in those days. Then someone saw him tanning on a towel. Tongues, tongues! Later a woman appeared, one wearing a trouser suit. Even more tongues!

The closer the showground, the smaller the houses, tiny squares with low roofs. Here people sat on wooden chairs by the back door, peeled vegetables, shelled peas, ducked back into the kitchen when the batch of rusks had to come out the oven. Here the smell of aniseed, stories and skeletons literally hung over the garden gate, eager to invite you inside.

At the end of the street, the showground. Here we danced in circles during the harvest festival, each with a red scarf. Also: here my foot slipped on the top step of the pavilion, it was during the annual athletics day – I had to play accordion for the White team – and as I rolled down the steps the accordion screamed Wheee!

every time I landed on my back. But I always returned; during the agricultural show the best chicken pies were sold in the show hall, warm, soft pot-bellied circles with slightly too-raw pastry (I suspect demand was too big to allow a proper bake) and a creamy filling smelling of cloves and nutmeg.

Next door was the tennis court. Here I once had to attend a tennis camp for an entire weekend. A short woman with manly hair and sinewy legs swore she'd cure me of the soupy serve. A machine that looked like a green oven spat a thousand balls at me. I hit each one of them into the street and was asked to leave on the second day. Next to the sinewy woman's bag was a brand-new towel. I took it and gave it to Knopieshoed Koos, our only tramp.

Next to the tennis court was a strip of dust, the jukskei courts. Dead space, keep going. On the next corner was a big house in a big garden. Christmas roses, rose bushes and a few gnomes made sure that everything that could have been pretty instead quarrelled with one another. Apparently there was lots and lots of money in this family, but they were never seen. The house attracted me, sadness hung there like clouds on a washing line. But I had to cycle past, there weren't any trees or other hiding places, only pain in an open, sunny garden where all the plants were at war.

There were trees further down the street, many more and much prettier than in any other street. On one of the corners was a semi-detached house, in the one half a teacher had lived a few years earlier. One evening a woman out strolling saw the teacher kiss a schoolboy through an open window. She didn't call the police but the minister. The boy finished matric in another town and the teacher disappeared. Then a thin man moved into the semi-detached. Every day he sat on the front porch and sharpened knives and yelled at everyone who went past, What are you looking at? Even when nobody was looking.

One afternoon, after another trip through town, I slowly cycle back home. I don't feel like my dead room, or the piano. Now that Father is studying and our money is finished, not even the willow can hide me any more. I have to help all the time, do chores, prove that my homework is done, I'm never left alone. Sally also comes less often to clean. Mother and I have constant run-ins, about anything, food, piano practice, pocket money, listening to the radio or turning off lights. I lean my little bicycle against the porch and go in the front door. Mother is standing in the hallway with a duster.

Where were you? she asks.

In town, I say.

It's Friday, she says, Your father will be here in an hour and nobody is helping me.

Waaaah! screams Erik in his room.

Mother walks to the room, I'm right behind her.

Erik is standing upright in his playpen. He wants to get out, but that's where he has to stay when there's nobody to watch him. He doesn't cry, he just screams.

Waaaah!

Play with your things, says Mother, Daddy will be here soon.

Waaaah!

Mother leans forward and slaps him on his bottom. It's a light slap, Erik won't even have felt it, but her cupped hand makes a thudding sound on his nappy. He gets a fright and is quiet for a moment. Then he begins to cry, head bowed with a river of tears.

Don't hit my brother! I say furiously.

What did you say? says Mother.

Don't hit him! I yell, You shouldn't hit a child! You hit everyone!

I'll raise my children as I see fit, says Mother.

I am beside myself. I have to say something horrible. I remember a word, I don't know what it means, but I know it's bad.

Whore! I scream. Then I turn around and run. I know I'm dead.

What did you say! Mother calls behind me, Wait till your father gets home!

I speed off on my little bicycle, down the untarred road, down the street, left, right, on and on. If the inhabitants of the last few houses were looking through their windows, they would see the shadow floating above me, a darkness with sharp points like the torn coat of a witch. I am at the dam. I get off my little bicycle and start dragging it up the wall.

The dam was just outside town, on one side were a few tall trees and an open area where people could park, the rest of the dam was embraced by a high wall full of plants trying their best to be reeds, thin tubes that could cut you badly when you forgot to push them out of the way.

I lie flat. Nobody will see me in the undergrowth. Shadow Three flaps around me.

Go away! I whisper.

Shadow Three stays. I lie without moving. I can never go back, they will kill me. What have I done? Where does that word come from? Did The Prince hear it? Did the house angel hear it? I am going to burn in the flames for ever and ever.

The sun is setting when I wake up. I can't see if Shadow Three has left. Hasn't anyone been looking for me? Didn't they want to do it here? Talented child beaten to death on dam wall, I could see it on every front page. Where do I go now? It's getting darker, in an hour the people who want to talk in secret come in their cars, the lamebrains smoking stinking zol among the cruel tubes, Mad Henry rowing his raft, do I want to die here or at home?

It's twilight when I push my little bicycle up the untarred road. I don't want anybody to hear me. Father's car is in front of the garage. I put my little bicycle away in the storeroom and creep across the porch to the front door. Father and Mother and Ian and

Erik's voices are in the dining room. I skulk through the sitting room, down the hallway into my dead room. I don't turn on the light, I get into bed in my clothes and with my dirty dam feet and bury my head under the pillow. After a minute I get out and straighten the bed again. I slide on my stomach underneath the bed.

The next morning I am woken by the lawnmower's drone. I forget I'm under the bed and hit my head hard on the planks. I cry a little and stay down. A few minutes later there is a knock at the door.

Come and eat your Post Toasties, says Mother, Then you can help your father pick up the grass.

I waited the entire day and the next day for my sentence and execution. There was nothing, nobody said a word. I was never hit again. Life went on as though nothing had happened. But there was an unease, Shadow Three lingered nearby like a transparent reproach (from whose side? Mine? Everybody's?), ready to turn the smallest squabble into a storm.

Forty years later I am a singer, often on my way to a performance at that exact moment when an afternoon starts to change colour and familiar shadows lose their shape. And still I see them, there among the last few houses before I have to turn off to a theatre, the stains that hang and duck, appear and disappear, with sharp points like the torn coat-tails of a witch.

Miss Snyman

If it hadn't been done ten years before in a movie, Miss Snyman would surely have descended from the sky in her long dress, long coat, hat, scarf, gloves, boots and umbrella; but she was one of the world's few true originals and thus decided on another arrival. She just appeared. Late one morning as we stood innocently in front of the art class in a disorderly line, she opened the door, stepped outside and pointed at the door with a gloved hand. One after the other we walked into the doorpost, nobody could look away, we kept staring at this woman. Somewhere someone must have left open a storybook and she simply escaped.

We tripped over our feet and stood around in a daze, nobody could remember where they usually sat, even the naughtiest children, those who could cause trouble in any circumstances, were quiet.

My name is Snyman, she said. (She never ever used the word 'surname'.)

Morning (mumble, mumble), Snyman, we said.

It's Miss, she said, But keep that for your other lessons, 'good morning' is sufficient. You are my first group, so first a necessary chore. Everyone pick up a chair, those closest to the door move first. Place your chair outside on the veranda, nicely against the wall so it doesn't bother anyone, then come back inside, don't fall over your question mark, an explanation awaits.

Five minutes later we're all back inside, in more of a daze than before. The chairs are all outside.

When we get the chance to explore our talents fully, we don't sit, says Miss Snyman, It is unhealthy and makes some of us extra stupid, we stand or we move. You are welcome to sit anywhere else on earth, just not here. To start, each of you will use the work surface closest to him or her. Very soon you'll find it is not the right place for you, then you'll look around until you think you know where you'll be able to work better, you go there and politely ask your classmate if you can swop places, nobody can refuse. So we keep on moving for a few weeks. I promise you that each of you will be at your best spot before the end of this year.

We are speechless.

Can anybody tell me why it's so hot in this room? asks Miss Snyman.

Fearless Jacques raises his hand.

Because it's summer, he says.

Miss Snyman smiles.

Here we have the first part of the answer, she says. Outside it is hot. Inside it is too hot. Because all the windows are open, as is the door. Thus the air moves too slowly, like when families eat too much at once. If we make sure that the door and the windows on both sides of the room are opened just a crack, the air will circulate better and faster, in other words, we create a draught. Shall we try?

We push the windows closed until only a chink is open.

Better? she asks.

We nod. We can't feel any difference at all, but the idea is so exciting and makes so much sense, we begin to believe that this new woman can do anything. She doesn't even feel temperature, it's high summer and she's covered from head to toe.

Time to work, she says. Think about it, every morning there is a distance between you and the school, no matter where you live and how you eventually get to school, and what you notice on your way here influences your mood. Today, each one of you will give this careful consideration and then depict what would make you the happiest. What do you want to see every day on your way here?

We don't move a hair. Eventually Jacques puts up his hand again.

What should we use? he asks, Our other teacher always said crayons or pencils or powder paint.

Let's hope she's happy where she's now, says Miss Snyman. No one may tell an artist what he's allowed to use, now and then we'll concentrate on a specific material to discover its many uses, but today we have to find happiness. Your eyes and your hands should itch, your heart should sing, look around you, somewhere there is something that wants to jump into your arms. Use it! Open the cupboards, remember there's also charcoal and clay and ink and starch and plaster of Paris and glue and sand and paper. Cut carefully, if you bleed you bleed outside.

Chaos. Suddenly we are feverish kittens in a sandbox. We grab everything we can. Every now and then we look behind us. Miss is at her table, calmly taking books from a big, embroidered bag. Nobody is going to stop us, nobody is going to yell, Put that back! or Not that drawer!

I remember there are big rolls of paper in the tall cupboard. The teachers use it to make bazaar posters. I grab a big roll and roll it open on the workbench. I also remember that I've seen tubes of paint in a drawer, these are only used by the bigger children, the rest of us have to make do with the powder paint. I know you can dilute this with water and mix the colours you want. I pour water into a jar and choose three paintbrushes from a tall container. There is a stack of thin boards on which you can squeeze out and mix paint. I start with black paint. With the finest brush I paint the outlines of big flowers. The whole poster full. Then I begin colouring in the pollen circles and leaves with a bigger brush. With each flower I get wilder, every petal is another colour, the pollen goes from yellow to pink to purple, green stems become blue, others get white and blue stripes like sailors' jerseys. The background I paint a deep blue. Despite our breezy new classroom

I prefer the winter, getting up early is awful, but it is very special to go to school in the dark.

Without a word Miss Snyman walks around the classroom. Next to me is Estelle. In front of her lie two wooden blocks, a ball of wool and a pile of feathers. She stares at it. Miss Snyman comes to a stop.

Any plans? she asked.

I don't know what I want to do, says Estelle.

That's one of the characteristics of a good artist, says Miss, A lovely torment, frustration and obstruction. Scream a little, it always helps.

Hoo-ee, Estelle whispers.

Butterflies scream better, says Miss. Class, I think we all need to help this young lady. Close your eyes, shake your heads and scream until all the frustration is out!

Haaaaah! we scream. So loudly that we get a fright.

Again! says Miss.

Haaaaaaaaah! we yell. It is wonderful.

Then someone pushes open the door. The school principal, a thin man with a rock-hard pompadour, stands there, obviously mystified.

This gentleman has come to see why our class is so lovely and cool, says Miss, And he wonders how we call up the power of creation. Shall we show him?

We scream as loudly as we can. Haaaaaaaaah! The principal disappears and closes the door behind him. Miss Snyman cracks it open again.

Art class became the highlight of the week. A frequent highlight! Finally! Thank you, thank you! Once a week Miss De Rotterd clipped my young soul's wings, once a week Miss Snyman made them whole. I stopped trying to fit in, I abandoned the morning ritual of standing around and being pushed around, I waited next to the hall in the courtyard until Miss Snyman appeared. Her outfits were unbelievable, where did you find clothes like that? Who would make them? Long coats of velvet or other fabrics that ordinary people would only wear at night or to weddings, dresses embroidered with tulips or peacocks or patterns that looked like the galaxy. Low-heeled boots in unusual shapes, gloves of thin leather, wool, fine crochet yarn, scarves in bright colours, scarves in dark colours, jewellery that consisted of fine chains or shoelaces or strings of gemstones with objects hanging from the bottom, miniature marionettes, faces or tassels.

And the hats. Miss Snyman came the year before television appeared in every house in town. We didn't know yet that the British had already tortured a classic headpiece into the befeathered, beleaved, beribboned beetles that today still disfigure women's heads worldwide. In those days a hat covered the head properly, framed a face, accentuated a neck and completed the outfit of an elegant or eccentric woman. Miss Snyman was the only woman left in the universe capable of wearing this very tricky accessory. She didn't miss a step and had no equal – any day, any place or time; it was something to see.

And she saw me looking. She saw that I tried to fly every time she glued back a wounded wing between my shoulder blades. She encouraged me without saying a word, left me alone without walking away, captivated me like a play and kept on surprising me.

A child, even one older than ten, is still small and still experiences things primarily physically. Every day has so many setbacks and attacks that general knowledge often becomes a casualty. Only after a month or two do I discover that Miss Snyman has moved into our old house. One day she asks me and two other boys if we can help her after school, she's busy with a project at her home, it's not often that she'll say something like this but we should wear our ugly clothes.

Three o'clock that afternoon we are standing in her street. The house still looks the same. In front of the house is a massive dark-blue car. Not as old as Mr Olivier's Pontiac, but still from an era before my birth. Miss Snyman appears in a long overcoat with big buttons like a butcher's, rubber gloves and a straw hat with a ribbon the same colour as the car. She looks at our ugly clothes and bare feet and smiles. She opens the back door of the car and the three of us get in. We sit in silence as she drives out of town, she doesn't take one of the main street's two exits but drives down a narrow untarred road that starts once we're past the school and dormitory. I don't look out the window very often, I look at the straw hat and the two rubber gloves on the big, old-fashioned steering wheel, a picture I will never forget.

We stop next to a stream. We get out and Miss Snyman opens the boot. Inside she has spread out a big blanket.

We are going to pack it full of pebbles, she says, Each as big as the palm of your hand, each nice and smooth. The wet ones you can bring to me first, I'll dry them. And you don't have to look around, we have permission to be here. You only need permission when your plans begin inside another man's borders.

Ninety minutes later the boot is full of pebbles from the river. My belief that nothing is impossible for Miss Snyman is firm, but I wonder if we'll ever be able to move with this load. We get in and Miss places her gloves on the steering wheel. We drive back to town as though we've loaded the boot with the feathers of a single chicken. At the house we each grab a few pebbles and follow her to the front door. She pushes the door open. I can't believe my eyes. The Five Holes Of The Constant Chord is now a golden sphere filled with planets, moons, stars, water, leaves, mermaids and other unfamiliar beings, painted in oranges, yellows and browns against a golden background, across the whole floor, up the walls and fading gradually across the ceiling as though there is a hidden exit.

In the sitting room the wooden floor has been sawn away at the four corners, four triangular holes are waiting there.

The pebbles go in the corners, says Miss, You can just carry them inside.

She folds a small blanket in front of the first triangle and sits back on her heels. She takes off the straw hat, her hair has been braided with ribbons into a soft formation on top of her head. She packs the first pebbles and looks around at us. We swallow hard and run back to the car.

An hour later the sitting room's corners have been filled with river pebbles. They haven't been stacked neatly or levelly so you can walk on them, they look like they've ended up there by themselves, unusual triangles filled with different shades of light grey. The wooden floor now looks as though it is outside, an eight-cornered landing strip for an unknown craft.

Gentlemen, I will thank you with tea and biscuits I learnt to make far from here, says Miss.

We follow her to the kitchen. I can't believe I ate here with Father and Mother and Ian and Erik, everything is unrecognisable. (With every visit the house was different, even the golden sphere was soon replaced by a snow-white calm.) We sit at the table. Miss holds out a square side-plate full of biscuits. I take a biscuit, it looks and smells like a ginger biscuit, but it is soft, inside are raisins, chopped peel and glacé cherries. I have never tasted anything like this. She pours tea into small cups. Boys of eleven seldom want tea, but we are as good as gold, it wouldn't surprise anyone to find out that she can cast spells. On the table are two small pots with sugar and tiny silver spoons. I pull a pot closer and put three teaspoons of sugar in my tea. Miss appears from the kitchen. I take a big gulp of tea. It's salt! The little pot is filled with salt! Who puts salt in a pot?

Another biscuit? asks Miss.

I shake my head. I don't know what to do. Drink, stupid, drink. I take two big gulps. I jump up.

My mom is waiting, I say, Thanks, Miss.

In front of the library I throw up like a carnivore that's caught something much too big.

Who puts salt in a pot? I ask at home. Mother laughs.

Some people, she says, The arty ones and the chefs. But you like everything that's bohemian, don't you. We all learn. Have more water. You'll feel better just now.

Decades later, family members of Miss Snyman tracked me down. They'd read in an article how much I admired her and how much she had influenced me. Apparently she spent her last years in the old-age home across the road. (I can only imagine how she must have turned that place upside down! How lucky were those who experienced her!) Apparently she'd been in Argentina before she landed in our midst. From Argentina to Porterville? Snyman? I can only say a prayer to the angels that after my death I too will still make someone wonder. There can be no greater legacy.

Friday, Saturday, Sunday

At least once a month we were packed into the church hall like sardines. This was the era of tours. Plays, scenes from the Bible, choirs, fat men in red waistcoats with instruments from the Eastern bloc, gymnasts, small circuses, recitations, any individual or group with a van or a bus could park behind our stage and put on a show. The moment a troupe left town the posters were taken down and the windows washed, within days new posters appeared and everybody began to caucus. Are we going? Is it suitable for children? What does the minister say? Does the verger know anything? Who phoned to book the hall? How much are the tickets?

The hall was either filled to the brim or completely empty, decisions were taken collectively: the town either embraced visitors and their talents or continued with its monthly roster as though nobody had come knocking. The hall was never half-full. This small-town culture still rules: an artist is either a hero or dead on arrival.

The most popular event was Lida Meiring's annual visit. This remarkable woman with her powerful voice and amazing energy put on a new play every year; I remember these as being one-man shows. Was there another performer on stage? We didn't notice him or her at all. With titles like *As Miempie kom kuier* and *As Miempie troukoors kry*, she made sure we'd be talking about the tour de force for weeks, for months we'd be repeating her one-liners. The days beforehand were unbearable, the hall was full an hour before the show, you could see they were still bustling about behind the curtain, we were much too early, but we were done waiting.

Then the lights were turned off, never dimmed but turned off one by one like in a factory after six. The curtain was raised and a few doors stood in their frames. I remember the doors, there were always doors, mop in hand she stormed in through one, we were hysterical. Then she and the mop vanished and a second later she stormed back through another door as a new character, mop on the head. I, who to this day do not know how to laugh out loud, bellowed. Tears rolled down my neck, she was the funniest person alive. All town traumas, family troubles, school worries or money problems disappeared, four hundred people were pain-free and happy. This happiness stayed with us for weeks.

Then the first music revue appeared. This was at a time when debates and church services were dedicated to the dangers of pop music and Satan's hidden presence in the throbbing beat. As soon as a new song was played on the radio, the most ordinary of people turned into prophets with long noses and crooked fingers, suspicious women dressed in black in Gaulish alleys a hundred years before Christ.

This revue's poster gave a foretaste of sin with a picture of a mirror ball and a young couple dancing in bell-bottoms and shiny vests that showed their navels. The town buzzed and cautioned and tickets were sold out weeks beforehand. Every night I stood in front of the mirror and looked for my own navel.

If anyone wondered where the expression 'On the big night . . .' came from, I can say with certainty that it was the Friday night of the music revue. I can't remember if our entire family was present or if it was just me and one or both parents; the image I have is of just myself in the front row of the gallery. One by one the lights died, jerkily the verger winched open the curtain. A pulsing rhythm filled the hall and then we were floating among the stars. Round and round the heavens turned. A big mirror ball hung in the centre of the stage, two strong spotlights shone on it from the back corners of the hall. The set was a light-blue arena of cardboard curls. Everything was covered in glitter. There were two singers, a young man and a girl, both in blue bodysuits, both covered in glitter, even their eyelids and cheeks were pasted with glitter. They sang while two couples danced, everyone in tight-fitting clothes, everyone slathered in oil and glitter, everyone with visible navels. Later someone blew fire, a girl in a silver evening gown sang on a tall stool, one couple danced a waltz dressed in clothes from Spain, the one who had been blowing fire earlier conjured doves from a hat, the mirror ball never stopped. After the finale the entire company ran off the stage, then back, then off again, then back again.

The curtain jerked shut. Our hands were sore from clapping, we were worn out, all our emotions drained. How would anybody ever sleep again? Where were the revue people going to sleep?

They would have to get naked to wash off all that glitter, where were they going to do that? Were we bewitched? Could you carry on living without a mirror ball? How long would I have to wait before I could have my own?

I didn't want to move. I stayed in my seat until the gallery was empty. From far away someone called my name. Come along! I got up and walked to the stairs. Slowly and unwillingly I went down the stairs, step by step. Like a thunderstorm that comes without warning, the growl was suddenly there. A low growl from the belly of the earth. A few people were still in the lobby, their lips moved but there were no sounds. Only the deep, deep groaning. The bottom of the staircase slowly began to curl upwards, nothing cracked or broke, I was in the middle of a calm, curling wave.

A second later I was behind the curtain. I was surrounded by the revue company. One dancer looked at me, his beard peeked through the glitter, his stomach had fine wrinkles. The girl's lipstick was smeared and she looked down, her dress's seam was working itself loose, threads hung to the floor. The singer turned around to walk away, inside the bodysuit his buttocks were long and loose like those of the rugby coach in the blue tracksuit. Someone began moving the décor, the shiny arena was full of cracks, paint peeled and the peaks of the curls were bumpy, the layers and layers of glue and glitter sat like foam.

Then the staircase lowered, the last step slotted back in place on the floor, the growl went quiet and the people in the lobby got their voices back.

Well, I don't know, said a woman, It's nice, but it leaves you a bit uncomfortable.

After the revue things were never the same again. I couldn't stop thinking about the mirror ball. How lovely everyone was while it turned, how horrible when it stopped.

But there is one of those at the skating rink! said the neighbours' youngest son after I'd told him about the revue.

Unlike in many other towns, our church wasn't in the high street, only the church hall was. And on a corner. On the opposite corner was the garage where my father used to work before he started studying. On the corner on the other side of the road was a clothes shop. Here everybody bought church shirts and ties. Right next to the clothes shop was the Slab of Intrigue. This was disguised as a roller-skating rink. On Saturday evenings the owner of the café (the café was built onto the back of the clothes shop) mounted loudspeakers outside the back windows and played loud music, not loud enough to upset the minister (the parsonage was next to the church hall), just loud enough to attract awakening hormones from every block.

The Slab of Intrigue was the town's leveller. On this cement slab, fenced with signboards advertising cooldrinks, all financial success, sporting achievements, academic honours and family history vanished. Children who during the week were kept in the shadows by self-consciousness, acne or cigarettes, on Saturday evenings stepped onto the slab in make-up, leather jackets and hair gel. Those who despised sport paraded here with muscled arms and long, lean legs in stretch denim. Those who were mistreated at home and shyly endured the daylight ruled here as young tigers. Influential, untouched and outgoing schoolgirls here humbly awaited the attention and instructions of the town's true leaders, the disreputable, irresistible studs of the slab. The ritual of standing around and sneaking glances with cans of Iron Brew in hand lasted several hours before the first roller skates were laced up.

A few coloured light bulbs were fastened beneath the café's gutters. In one corner was a small mirror ball, so badly lit that only a few pale measles shimmered on the café's wall. A single wire with yellowish light bulbs lit the slab. No beauty, no glory. Only a café with a cement slab. But here drama lurked and plots were hatched. The Slab of Intrigue drew dark thoughts and forbidden desires from body and mind, pulled them through the walls into this cocoon of raw power – the wonderful phase when young lions can't tell the difference between playing and fighting.

One Saturday evening I arrive here with the neighbours' youngest son. He hires a pair of roller skates, I have mine under my arm. These were my Christmas present the year before and – after I had skinned every possible body part during a few experiments in our empty garage – ended up in the storeroom. But I am here with my skates, the attraction of a mirror ball is much greater than my fear of blood or embarrassment. We each get an Iron Brew and take a seat on one of the long benches.

Where is the mirror ball? I ask.

Right above your head, he says.

I look up. The measles ball turns slowly against the wall. Half of the mirror tiles have dropped off. For a moment every child on earth forgets every fairy tale ever told. Everything that is beautiful is now forgotten. I am pink and weak and I cannot skate.

I'm going home, I say, You have to walk with me.

Are you mad? says the neighbours' youngest son. We're here now.

I'm going to fall, I say.

You just hold on to something, he says.

To what?

The worm?

What worm?

Only the prince and the princess skate alone. And the king and the witch and the murderer. The rest make a worm or a dragon. They're working on a story because they want to put on a skating show one day. You just hold on to the one in front of you. Nobody falls.

I put on my skates. I hold on to the bench, to the neighbours' youngest son, the fence, the handrail and then Thomas Redelinghuys. He was a quiet child in the support class who sat next to the one who had unzipped his trousers. He had olive skin and long pitch-black lashes. And lips like a mannequin. He was prettier than any girl in the district. The Winded Woman once said that pretty boy and his beautiful father were like coach wheels, shiny and golden and not yours.

Thomas is the worm's second-last pair of legs, I am right at the back. I'm holding on to his waist. His body is rock hard, I can feel things moving on the inside, muscles or skeleton, things I've never felt before.

'Touch me in the morning,' Diana Ross whispers over the loud-speakers. The worm starts moving. The neighbours' youngest son said nobody falls, but when the worm starts to curl around the first corner my feet are crossed, I don't know why, I didn't lift them once. I am on my knees, then my stomach, but I don't let go. At the next turn the whole worm falls down. There is a streak of blood behind me. The neighbours' youngest son walks me home, my knees burn like they're on fire. I give him my skates, he says thank you, but they're too small.

Three weeks later, on a Sunday afternoon, we are sitting in a tent in the middle of our massive lawn, the neighbours' youngest son and I. Sunday afternoons were the worst time of the week, I remember the obstinate heat, the boredom (finished reading, finished writing to Grandmother, finished tidying), the wandering behind the sawmill next door, the climbing on stacks of wood, the smell of pinewood and oil, later the typical Sunday smell of warm fruit in the other neighbours' orchard. Even later I spend an eternity staring down the deserted street. There were no prospects, Sunday evening was snacks, Monday morning was school, a desperate time!

Then the tent appeared. From where? We didn't have money for big expenses. The tent had a pitched roof like a house in a drawing and was big enough for two children's sleeping bags. At the top in the middle was a rolled-up length of canvas that you could untie and let hang like a wall between two rooms.

The neighbours' youngest son and I sit on either side of the canvas.

Are your knees still sore? he asks.

No, I say.

You're a late bloomer, he says, Everyone says so.

What's that? I ask.

You're a little slow, he says, Your head is still full of fairies, everyone says so.

Slow? I ask, What do you mean? I am twelve! No other child gets as many book prizes as I do!

Slow is slow, he says, Not with school things, with sex things.

Shhh!

I don't know what it means, but I know it's bad. I crawl out of the tent and check the house. I crawl back in.

You can't say things like that, I say, People get the death penalty.

For murder, yes, he says, Not for sex. Everyone does it.

What?

Sex stuff.

I say, I don't know what sex stuff is.

It's like playing Doctor Doctor, he says, Just worse.

How much worse? I ask.

The man lies on top of the woman, he says.

Why? I ask.

They make waves, he says, Like at the dam or by the river. The man takes his dragonfly and then he stirs the woman's pool.

Where's that? I ask.

The neighbours' youngest son lifts up the canvas and shows with his hand.

Sis, man! I yell. I am angry and excited. I tremble.

How else do people have babies? he says, How do you think a woman gets pregnant?

From the swelling, I say.

From the going into the pool, he says, Everybody does it.

My parents would never do it, I say, We're always at home.

They wait until you're asleep, he says, Up and down, up and down, ooh nice, ooh nice!

Out of my tent! I say, Go back home!

Late bloomer, he says.

I hear him walk away. Then I crawl outside. I pull the pegs from the grass. The tent collapses. I leave it right there. I walk to the willow and for the first time in a long while I sit beneath the dome. I will never come out of here again. I will never talk to anyone again. Pigs. They're all pigs. I know the neighbours' youngest son is right. I always knew people did things like that. But I never knew that's where I came from. I thought I'd been sent.

Rod

Paarl's drive-in theatre announces that it is presenting a special Rod Alexander weekend. For two nights in a row it will show his two hit movies from the previous year, *Aanslag op Kariba* and *Snip en Rissiepit*. Both movies on both nights.

A detailed agenda is drawn up. Saturday morning the expedition heads off to Wellington. Grandmother makes lunch. This is followed by a short nap before we leave for Magdel's home. Her mother has bought a new single, we have been invited over for a listen and coffee. Then an early bath and the drive to Paarl for a good parking spot and the double show. Then a sleepover and breakfast. Thick slices of raisin bread! Soft butter! Soft scrambled eggs! Yoghurt with preserved guavas! (Sometimes Grandmother winked and said, Oh, the yoghurt is finished. Then we got custard!) Then back in time for the evening service – missing the morning service is already a big scandal.

We stop in front of Grandfather and Grandmother's little house. Chicken pie with golden, flaky pastry, carrots with honey and cinnamon, baked beans, potatoes roasted in lard, herb rice, fritters with yellow cheese, confetti salad and pancakes with peach syrup. We've barely said hello and Grandmother is already carrying the offerings to the table. Even in those years we knew it was unhealthy to lie down right after a meal, but nobody has a choice, we are as limp as farm flies.

At half past three we leave for Magdel's home. I have to preach to myself: I am always a little cross when we go there. I envied them their big house and the fact that they could live so close to Grandmother, how many adventures did I miss? (Recently Magdel told me about a time Grandmother had to babysit them and tried to put them to sleep by reading them a *Huisgenoot* article about Rudolf Hess's horrific deeds.)

Don't, says Grandfather.

Grandmother is tying a dishcloth around a plate.

Don't, says Grandfather, It's only four minutes away.

Who drives without provisions? says Grandmother. What if the car breaks down?

Then we walk, says Grandfather.

Ian and I go with Grandfather and Grandmother in the grey Beetle. Erik goes with Mother and Father. Up the hill.

Why does Magdel have such a big house? I ask.

Because you have such a big garden, says Grandmother. Everyone on earth has something and needs something. So we become happy and so we stay humble.

That was true. I couldn't argue.

But why do they live in Wellington?

Because Chris works with fruit, says Grandmother, He's very clever at work.

Magdel's father was high up in the Dried Fruit Council. That was true. I couldn't argue. With a new-found serenity I walk up the steps to the front porch. In the big sitting room we all sit in a semicircle. Magdel's mother lifts the needle of the record player and places it on the new seven single. Kris Kristofferson sings 'Why Me, Lord'. Afterwards it's quiet. A few wipe away tears.

He sounds like his cough syrup is finished, says Grandmother, How is it possible that a man who sings so badly can make me feel so sad? Play it again.

He sings again. More tears. Coffee and lamingtons. Erik, Ian, Lanie and Bennie run screaming around the house. Magdel shows me her new books. Everyone is called in for a photo. We sit in a semicircle again. Then down the stairs, down the hill. We have a bath and put on our pyjamas.

Why do we have to see a movie in pyjamas? I ask.

It will be late when we get back, says Mother, I'm not going to try to dress sleeping children then.

That's stupid, I say, People will laugh when we get out.

The man with the food comes to the car, says Grandmother.

I had forgotten. The highlight of the evening at the drive-in, the man with the tray and the leather strap round his neck. Bar One! KitKat! Tex!

Ask him for polony, says Grandfather.

Where is the polony? I ask.

He sticks the polony to his stomach, says Grandfather, It stays there because of the sweat, he just opens his shirt and then you pick a slice.

Sis, Ben! says Grandmother.

We shudder and laugh. Grandfather doesn't laugh. He's told us many times how grown-ups lie to children. He only tells the truth.

We arrive at the drive-in, pay at the big gate, there aren't many cars yet, we get a good spot right in the middle. Father winds down the window, hooks the speaker over the glass and winds the window back up. I sit in front next to Father, Mother sits in the back with Ian and Erik. Erik will fall asleep as soon as the cartoons are finished. Mother hands us Grandmother's plate with the dishcloth.

Eat now while it's still light, she says, Else there will be stains everywhere tomorrow.

On the screen advertisements appear. Slides with faded photos of local businesses: butcheries, bakeries, petrol stations. Then the cartoons follow, then black-and-white news, Jim Fouché poses in front of a new hospital and John Vorster opens the parks in Johannesburg to all races.

Here comes trouble, says my father.

No, it's only a short interval, says my mother.

Are they bringing the chocolates now? I ask.

No, only after the first movie, says my father.

Go slowly with the sweet things, says my mother, Your father's family all have bad teeth. One day you won't get a girlfriend.

I decide to ask for polony. I don't want a girlfriend or bad teeth. Two of the dormitory boys' eyeteeth were pulled and now every-one calls them the beavers.

The first movie starts. There are terrorists, a dam wall, an angry woman and a thin man with a pitch-black moustache. It's boring and everyone wears ugly clothes.

How much longer? I ask.

It's only just started! says my father.

There he is, says my mother.

Rod Alexander appears on the screen. The people in the movie call him Beyers, but I know his name is Rod. I have seen him in many magazines and never taken much notice. But here he is now, metres tall on a screen surrounded by bright stars and a sickle moon. Despite his moustache he is more beautiful than anyone who's ever lived, more beautiful than the gold of Miss Snyman's wall, more beautiful than the cooing of all the doves in the Boland, more beautiful than the house covered in ivy at the Hugenote Kollege. His shirt strains across his chest, the button trembles like a pebble in a sling. I chew my dressing gown's belt into a wet ball.

What's happening now? my mother asks.

I'm not sure, says my father, He may be working with the crooks, we'll see now.

Ian is fast asleep, says my mother, But he'll wake up soon. And then he'll want to go to the bathroom.

I'll take him, says my father.

Quiet! I want to yell, but I keep on chewing my belt. I feel boxed in, I want to get away, I want to be with the terrorists, someone must capture me, someone must try to rescue me, we'll worry together, make plans, together we'll suffer and lose hope and then escape miraculously so we can talk about it for the rest of our lives.

At some point the movie comes to an end, I have long since stopped following the story, I have my own plans. INTERVAL appears in the centre of the empty screen. Father and Ian go to the bathroom, Mother sits with her eyes closed and Erik sleeps like a bag of cement. I'm not hungry, my head is full of possibilities, my stomach is full of butterflies, but I keep a lookout for the man with the tray. Later Father and Ian get back in the car. The screen goes dark. *Snip en Rissiepit* starts. Rika Sennett is gorgeous, Rod's moustache is gone and he is now even more beautiful than at the dam. They talk about things I don't understand, argue about things that go over my head, but I am glued to my seat, I cling to the dashboard, my forehead practically against the windscreen.

Someone knocks at Father's window. It's the man with the tray.

Does anybody want anything? Father asks.

No, I say.

There's no answer from the backseat, they're all asleep.

Not even a KitKat? asks Father.

Nothing, I say. I'm upset. Everything is wrong. The man is late. Father's talking disturbs the bubble in which I've been living. Now I am back in a car filled with family. Father buys something and eats it. The wrapper is noisy, I want to go insane.

Then the kiss arrives. Rod kisses someone. I don't know who. It's a kiss with open lips. Like when we practised in the sunroom. But now it's Rod who's kissing. Huge on the screen. Among the stars.

Bing! Our car's roof shoots off. Shoop! Shoop! Shoop! Shoop! Father, Mother, Ian and Erik shoot up into the air! Bing! Bing! Shoop! Shoop! Everybody's roofs shoot off. Everybody shoots up into the air. People hang motionless in the sky. Hundreds of bodies hang silently above Paarl. I am alone. Rod's mouth is open against the heaven.

The next morning I wake up on my mattress in Grandmother's sitting room. My body is heavy and tired, I am worn out, everything the angels gave me, everything sprinkled over me in the sandpit by mistake, it's all used up. The night before was almost too big. It was the first night that was mine alone, I saw and I felt how far I would have to reach, how far I would have to leave home behind. Maybe too young to properly put into words discoveries or suspicions, but somewhere a seed was planted: the vague possibility that some can only find a home under an unreachable ceiling.

After breakfast we say goodbye. I hold on tightly to Grandmother, I love her very much. But now I have to go back to the small town and the small existence. I drag my feet to the car. Back to the long wait for independence.

Location

It was the custom to start the schoolday with a short religious study period. First there was roll call, then the teacher read a piece from the Bible and then there was prayer. If there was enough time, we could ask questions or tell the class something.

It was a Tuesday or Thursday, the teacher with the brown jacket (Mondays and Wednesdays it was the blue one, Fridays the red one with one missing button; when I told Grandmother about this she said it was better to think of it as one extra buttonhole) read from Luke about the angel appearing to Mary to tell her she was going to give birth.

After prayer I raised my hand and asked when one of us was going to see an angel. She answered that I shouldn't take everything so literally.

I reminded her that angels are described everywhere in the Bible and also appear in paintings and on Christmas cards. How else was I supposed to take it?

She answered that religious study was about the Heavenly Father and not other beings.

I asked why we had to read about Moses and Aaron, in that case.

She closed her eyes (she always struggled to keep her temper for an entire sacred period) and the bell rang.

I was going through a phase of distrust. I was convinced that everybody was either lying or keeping quiet, at school, at church, at home, on the radio, everywhere. That afternoon I walked home and decided to uncover at least one truth a week.

Sally was sitting in the sun next to the house with a big plate of food on her lap. It looked nice, like when we ate outside on holiday in Langebaan or Franskraal. I stopped in front of her.

Why don't you eat inside? I asked.

I don't sit with the baas, Sally said.

I'd forgotten that my father was at home. The last few weeks he'd spent more time at home than at Stellenbosch. Another truth that had to be uncovered.

You often sit inside, I said, Come in, I'm also going to have lunch.

No man, sis, Sally said. For a moment – only for a moment – she, who was always cheerful, looked annoyed.

I walked into the kitchen. Everyone had finished eating. Mother was doing the dishes, Father was drying them, Ian was heatedly explaining to Erik that you paged through a book, you didn't tear or throw it.

Why doesn't Sally eat inside any more? I asked.

She eats where she wants to, Mother said, Go take off your school clothes, I want to do the laundry.

I have to take the cot apart, said Father.

What's happening to the cot? I asked.

It's going to Sally's home, Mother said, Erik is too big and apparently there's another little one in her family.

What if we get another baby? I ask.

I'm poor enough, Father laughed, We're finished.

And they took out my stork, Mother laughed.

I want to go too, I said.

Then get undressed, your clothes are on your bed, Mother said.

Fifteen minutes later we're driving down the high street. I'm sitting in front next to Father, Sally is sitting in the back, the boot is half-open and fastened with an elastic cord, the pieces of the cot peek out like garden railings. Just outside town we turn right onto an untarred road. It's the road to the location. Here the coloured people live. Father drives very slowly: in front of us is a bakkie that's sending a massive ball of dust into the air. Through the dust I can see there are five or six coloured men on the back of the bakkie, everyone sitting, one standing. He is dressed in a neat dark-grey suit with a white shirt and tie. He stands upright like a statue and holds on to the roof with one hand. He looks like a figure in an old painting, a respected man, the bearer of a shocking message.

Who's that? I ask.

It's the preacher at the mission church, says Father, He is a very clever man, he once addressed our church council.

The bakkie slows down, but doesn't stop. Two of the men jump down. One stumbles and falls forward. Father drives past the bakkie. The preacher doesn't turn his head or look at us. He stands as if in a painting. Driving the bakkie is a man with big red cheeks and a red nose covered in bumps. (That's a drinker's face, the Winded Woman always said when she saw a red one.) A cigarette sticks to his bottom lip. The seat next to him is empty.

Why doesn't he let the minister sit in front? I ask.

I don't know what other people's stories are, says Father.

He doesn't even stop when someone gets off, I say, He's rude!

I know I should keep quiet now, but I can't help myself.

I hope something happens to him! I say.

Hey! says Sally from the back.

You can't say things like that! says Father.

I keep quiet. We turn left onto Sally's street and drive into the location. I've been here only once before and I remember that I liked it. The streets were narrow and untarred, the houses were bitterly small, but neat, the fences were covered in sweet peas, tomatoes and peas with curly tendrils. Perhaps it was only Sally's street that was so pretty, perhaps it was some inherited way of looking at certain things, perhaps it was the wages of our sins, like Aunt Hamman said more than once, perhaps it was the shame that would follow us to our graves, like I heard the rich woman across the road say once without moving her lips. I didn't know what any of these things meant, from Sally eating outside to the preacher standing upright without looking away from the dust cloud to the rich woman's declaration, but the facts would come, one by one.

We stop in front of Sally's home, there are lots of people in the garden, her children, her sister, her mother, her brother. Father unties the cord and lifts out the cot pieces. Some of the family members come to help and carry the pieces into the house, others stay at the gate. They don't look at us, they look at each other or at the cot or at the sky or at the car or at the ground, but not at us.

Bye, Sally, I said.

Thank you, Sally says. She looks down and closes the gate.

We drive back on the untarred road. We are almost at the trees just outside the town. The bakkie races out of the last street and makes a sharp turn in front of us. We slam into its rear corner. Father jerks forward. My head hits the windscreen, hard. We come to a standstill. I don't know if the red man braked or yanked the bakkie's steering wheel, but it is now diagonally across the road and still skidding. With its front facing us it slides off the untarred road and hits a tree.

Father puts his hand to my forehead.

Are you okay? he asks.

I just got a fright, I say.

Father opens the door and runs to the bakkie. The red man struggles out the passenger door, he is short with dark-pink bandy legs and a thick neck. He bends forward, blood runs down his forehead.

I have had a big fright and now feel like throwing up. I turn my head away. I know I have to stop cursing others, I do it every time out of fear or anger, quickly, before I can even think about it. And every time the cursed one is hit by disaster. How am I going to stop? Especially now that I know I know nothing?

Mini

In the corner of the stage in the church hall, behind the curtain, stood a Bible. Made of wood by my father, one metre high with a slot on top. One afternoon a week it was pushed to the side of the stage near the steps. Then the majority of the town's children met for Kinderkrans. A few women supervised, my mother was one of them.

Every week those who wanted to could go up on stage and recite one or more Bible verses. After a successful recitation a page with the Bible verse and the child's name was slipped into the wooden Bible's slot. At the end of the year the pages were counted and the winner got a prize. I liked reading the Bible, it was easy to memorise and required me to appear on stage. It was a family affair, Father made the Bible, Mother taught the class and I won the prize.

One afternoon, Mother and I were once again on our way to Kinderkrans in the yellow Mini. This little car was bought out of necessity after Father's studies had begun. Mother, who'd been a teacher before my birth, had to go to work in the mornings to keep the wolf from the door. This job was at the crèche on a farm just outside town. Mother had to learn how to drive. It was a process of squeals, tears, outbursts, reproaches, refusal, quitting, restarting, rage, prayer and acceptance. Where she got her licence I have no idea. Our town had only one traffic official, every day he sat in his car, dead to the world, always with an open window, always in the high street, right across from the post office. Whether it was an unhappy marriage, the lack of actual traffic, alcohol or sleeping sickness, he was in no mood for being awake. If he was authorised to issue licences, Mother must have got hers here; if the passing-out ceremony took place in a bigger town it must have been during one of my holidays in Wellington – I was spared that trauma.

Mother was the world's most worried driver. Ian and I woke up in the morning and immediately pulled the curtains aside, it didn't matter how much the farmers needed it, we prayed that the rain would stay away. If it rained Mother would want to take us to school and it wasn't healthy for a child to fear for his life in primary school. Even though she and Erik had to drive past our school to get to the farm school, we preferred to walk. (To get to the farm, she had to cross a bridge without railings – a cement ruler. I suspect it was at this time, in the back of the Mini, that Erik began to shut his eyes and cultivate the gripping inner life he enjoys to this day.)

One afternoon Mother and I and the yellow Mini were on our way to the church hall for that week's Kinderkrans. It was close to the end of the year and I had memorised pages, it was my last chance to ensure my triumph. Over and over I said my lines.

Don't talk so loudly, Mother said, I'm driving.

Driving, like cycling, becomes second nature at some stage. The driver can listen to music, have a conversation or admire blossoms on a tree while actions are still taken and safe decisions are made. Not Mother: to her there was no logic to the workings of an engine or the sequence in which pedals, gears and indicators had to be used.

We always parked behind the hall. (Code: 'Part One of this horror now comes to an end. Don't even try to relax, you still have to get back home.') The hall was built on a slight incline and the double back door opened directly onto the stage. It was in front of this door that we always parked. This afternoon Mother was wearing a full skirt, not something that should have been a problem, but she always had to have a confirmed visual of a pedal before she stepped on it.

People often use the expression, My whole life passed before me. That is the truth. When you suspect your end is near your entire existence flashes before your eyes in the form of square photographs, in my case from right to left. We were just past the church, Mother forced the gearbox into a lower speed, the stage's double door materialised in front of us, the skirt was too full and she stepped on the accelerator.

Ebeeen! she screamed.

Nooooo! I screamed.

The Mini jerked to a halt with its nose against the door.

We could have died, I swallowed.

Nonsense, Mother said. But I could see her hand trembling.

That day I recited until there wasn't any more space for paper inside Father's wooden Bible. The next week I got the prize. (One of the neighbours' sons walked with me to the hall. He wasn't on his way to Kinderkrans, his cigarettes were finished.)

A week later I did get back into the Mini. Mother drove the three of us down the hill to the fold where the high street began to level out. Here a house stood, completely ordinary, struggling lawn, crooked wall next to the front porch, bright glass next to the front door, all the scars of the late fifties. We crowded into the sitting room, only Mother said hello, we sat down on the speckled carpet and didn't move or breathe for thirty minutes. In the corner was one of the first televisions in the country, test broadcasts had just begun. On the screen was a small Belgian detective, his name was Max. He drove along narrow alleys in a small European car to catch crooks. Afterwards we sat in a deathly silence for a few seconds. Then we jumped up.

Cooldrink?

No thank you, Auntie.

Thousands of pins lodged in my flesh. I looked around to see if Becca or Bora was there. The fidgeting that still courses through my body and ensures that I never sit still, that every day I walk ten kilometres around my dining-room table because I have an idea and too little time, as well as a madness that has become my bedfellow and makes me live without sleep, *that* I got on a speckled carpet.

We were out the front door before Mother could stop us. Suddenly we were glad to get into our Mini (not a little car any longer). Max has one, we have one! That weekend, after a short petition, I got my first driving lesson. It was easy, and Father and I and the Mini were up and down the untarred road next to our long lawn. Later Mother called from the porch, Petrol costs money!

We stopped in front of the garage.

Can I reverse next week? I asked.

I'm sorry I hit you, Father said.

I was immediately uncomfortable. I didn't like sentences like that. Even if it was to heal a wound. Family talks were too intimate, they made my throat close up.

You think you're doing the right thing and then the next day you think it was wrong, he said, I don't know any more what you're supposed to do, what used to be right is now wrong. Or the other way around. Try to help your Mother, she doesn't like getting angry either. Things are difficult.

The next week I was looking forward to the reversing, I just hoped he wouldn't talk about unexpected things again. But he did. Just as I parked in front of the garage. He said that we were going to move, he had to live closer to his classes, it wasn't right that he was so far away and Mother had to manage on her own. He said we were going to be much closer to the city, then he could live in the house with us and Mother could get a job that paid better.

I didn't care; except for my handful of friends there was little I would miss. My new fidgeting made me uneasy and maybe in a new place I could find out what to do with my many plans.

A few weeks later we drive out of town. Right at the front is the truck with all our belongings. Then the station wagon with Father and Ian and Erik. Bringing up the rear are Mother and I in the Mini. On my lap is a jam roll wrapped in waxed paper. Aunt Hanekom had baked it and sadly pushed it into my hands at the farewell.

The drive feels like an eternity. I cannot relax or look around, the road is quiet and Mother drives well, I don't trust the peace. We go past Saron, past Gouda, we turn right onto a bigger road. Cautiously I begin to look around, there are hills and train tracks, I recognise these from all the times we've driven to Wellington. But at one point we have to take a new road towards the city.

What is that? Mother asks anxiously.

What? I ask.

That red light? Mother says.

It's a robot, I say, Miss says the correct language is traffic light.

I'm not driving to there, Mother says, Your father didn't say anything about a traffic light.

We stop on the shoulder of the road. She flashes the lights of the Mini. I can see Father stopping ahead of us. Then the truck. The station wagon turns back and stops next to us.

Are we having jam roll now? I ask.

Father speaks through the window.

Just stay behind me, he says.

I'm not driving on strange roads, says Mother.

We're not going to drive on strange roads, says Father, We're driving to Wellington. We're leaving the Mini with Grandmother. Then all of us go together. I can fetch it tomorrow.

In Wellington we stop behind Grandmother's little house. We eat jam roll and drink coffee from the tall pot. Then we drive again, another whole hour. The new place is a labyrinth, so many streets, so many houses, we have to turn around a few times and start searching again. Both Father and Mother have said it hundreds of times, but I still can't remember the place's name, I who can recite almost the entire Bible.

Later we turn up a street and see the parked truck. We stop and look at our new home. There are only a few plants, the soil is sandy, the other houses are very close, the gardens are small, here and there someone is in front of or next to a house, some don't even look up. The truck's back door is open, our furniture looks frightened in this strange land. Father and Mother get out, Father talks to the people from the truck, Mother walks to the front door, Ian and Erik rush past her into the house. I stay in the station wagon, suddenly I feel completely insignificant. Hopelessly naïve. How will I survive here? I sit. Mad, mad, mad with nerves.

10 January 1978

It is the start of my third year in high school, we have been living in Kuils River for two years. There are now four children in the family: our little sister is thirteen months old. Her arrival was a miracle, without a stork Mother couldn't fall pregnant, but she did. At home we were like different people, it felt as though we'd received an order, we had to protect a rarity, a priceless and remarkable doll had been left with us, the world was too dirty and too dangerous. There were no instructions, we had to make our own weapons and come up with fresh strategies. Every morning we got up and stared at her, every afternoon we crept into the house and stared at her. Mother said the carpets were going to last forever, we were practically tiptoeing. Father stopped studying and began working again, we had to remodel the house, an extra room was needed. The garage was converted into a bedroom and bathroom – this was mine, brand new with fashionable brown walls and paintings of my favourite composers – and a new garage was built.

Inside my head a hurricane was creating both order and confusion; I was overloaded with information. Our new place had access to shopping centres, museums, churches, galleries, libraries, theatres, films and architecture that made me feel as though I'd never seen anything before. By that time there was also a television set in practically every home. There was no filter or sieve, I watched what I should and devoured what I shouldn't. I brought home every LP from the town library and put it on my turntable, late at night I lay with my ear pressed to the speaker, the universe of what had already been produced, in sound, in images and in words, was astonishing. It raised me up and brought me down, I stood on clouds and declared myself, every morning I was born a new leader, every afternoon I expired in clouds of doubt. I began losing interest in my schoolwork, my marks were low or average, I was confronted and questioned. I wanted to answer with my own questions: Don't you see anything? Doesn't anybody hear what's being sung and said?

Routine was the protector of the ordinary, a merciless guard that kept on screaming: On time! Late! Faster! Ahead! I was astonished at how satisfied people were, I couldn't help but see how each day they went back to homes that looked like all the others, how lawns were mutilated for the sake of order, how ugly cars were washed and washed, how a worn-out shirt was replaced with another one in the same style and colour. As if the first hadn't been bad enough, this second puberty was painful, like a young dragon growing an extra tail, also extra claws, extra talons, invisible to others, but painful enough to keep him aggressive. There are those who ask questions without questioning, those who are influenced but never inspired, those who teach but only see the obvious, those who look around in jealousy but seldom experience motivation; among them a young dragon has to swallow his flames and hide his extra growths and keep on believing a space is being saved for him, as well as the day when he can unfold his claws in this space, stretch out the talons from their bleeding holes, spit and stiffly rise from the ground.

By this second day of the new school year I had changed beyond recognition from the anxious, plump child in the back of the station wagon. I'd lost my primary-school fat, for the first time I had a narrow waist (this narrow waist I later girdled like a Victorian lady, my trademark at the start of my career), my legs had already begun to take a shape that elicited quick looks from some, my face was an unusual oval with eyes that could make an annoying classmate fall into an uncomfortable silence, my hair had lost its soft curl and was now a ghostly shock from an early rock opera. I had already learnt to buy my clothes – also school uniform – in smaller sizes or to alter standard sizes to accentuate or change what I wanted to.

Doubt and anger still simmered just below my skin. High-school pupils, some already worldly wise, others merely the products of their barren educations or entirely lost in the group culture, could prattle on without end. Like a knot of snakes on a warm rock, there was a group every few steps from which phrases kept escaping: No, I only learnt that page! My brother says they always ask that formula! Only the A candidates were called! They say the list of prefects has already been drawn up!

Again and again these little bombs shot my confidence to pieces. Pedagogues and books used words like growing up, adolescence, growing pains, awakening, perception, breaking down and building up; I read all of it. One thing became clear, not a thing I would ever find reassuring, just a fact: fear was paralysis, a monster that wrapped its tentacles around you, mangled your beliefs and coloured your judgement. But this never stopped me from implementing a plan or making an attempt. A merciful gift, also a massive burden. Forty years later, during the umpteenth opening night, I would still hide in my dressing room, crying and throwing up, before walking onto the stage ten minutes later and feeling the calm wash over me.

High school had a hierarchy: there were those who tried, those who achieved, those who were already fully developed physically, those still enfolded in innocence, those who were already sexually active, those who waited in silence for their freedom, those who had to flee horrible households, those who were heroes on the sports grounds. Despite the identical clothing, roles and physical formations, you could spot the ranks of this social order from an airplane. After break everyone had to stand in rows, girls on one side, boys on the other, arranged according to age and class group. I was seldom in a row, the closeness was too warm and unpleasant. I was usually on the veranda in front of the music class, on my way to a lesson. (Or just pretending that there was a lesson.) I kept watching: for a moment there was little movement, then everybody began moving involuntarily like chess pieces on a magnetised board. New rows were formed: the smokers, the achievers, the favourites, the gangs, the bullies, the innocents, the indifferent ones, the poisonous ones, the believers, the stupid ones, it was a game and a revelation.

The veranda in front of the music class was both a mercy and a terror. Finally I was in the hands of a music teacher who could see me. She believed in my talent and spent hours on my development. I worshipped and feared her. I practised like a machine, played advanced pieces, loved the sound, hated its theory. It was difficult, I was often discouraged, but didn't want to disappoint; she took me to concerts, brought me books and LPs, showed and taught me much more than what was prescribed in any curriculum, invited me to her home, taught me to play the organ, entered me in competitions and exams, let me perform in concerts and later let me accompany the school choir. I had extra lessons in the morning before school and in the afternoon after school. Music filled my days; I couldn't describe or explain it, I kept on hearing other things, words and sounds that were at odds with what I already knew, but for now it was the piano.

This was why I still wandered the school corridors on the second day of my third year in high school: I was trying to figure out my music timetable, it kept clashing with certain classes and there were other periods I wanted to fill. I'd decided I was done with nonsense like cadets, guidance, physical education, rugby and athletics. With and without permission I had already started various projects the year before, a drama group, an art group, décor for the library, pot plants for the lobby, a few friends were always ready for a new undertaking, teachers were used to seeing me in the corridors with a file or a pile of books.

I was standing in the second lobby – down the corridor from the school's front lobby there was another lobby where three corridors met, four glass doors led outside and the big staircase to the upper storey began. Two teachers walked past. The one was the zombie who taught something like geography at the end of the corridor, the other was the Adonis who taught English: high cheekbones, square jaw, thick hair like in a dubbed movie. He looked at me.

I hope I'm seeing you in class today, he said.

My heart left its usual spot and began bouncing through my entire body. His voice belonged to The Prince. Not as deep as the other times, also with more breath, but it was familiar after so many years. I didn't answer, I was struck dumb and my hands were clammy. He disappeared down the corridor. He was here, in one of his many guises, he was my new English teacher and I hadn't been in his class the previous day, I had been roaming with my timetable.

I looked up. There was a big window on the landing. Through the window you could see the roof of the bathrooms. On the roof the giant stood and looked at me. At the end of the previous year workers had begun repairing or retiling the school's roof, I could never see exactly what was happening, but every time I looked up, he was there. The giant was a big man with a caramel skin like someone from a Latin country. He was pretty with flames in his eyes and pitch-black hair, the ends sticking to his neck. Unlike the other workers he didn't wear an overall, he was barefoot, dressed in a white vest and shorts so tight that even looking was an embarrassment. I had never seen such legs, such a chest, such arms, he was a statue. I couldn't understand why he hadn't been reported. When the corridors were crowded with children he wasn't to be seen, but when one of us was walking alone, he was there. He stared, provocative, not moving. Like now.

This time I'm staring back. For two reasons: I decided I would.

And I have just recognised The Prince. We stand there. The giant and I.

The growl gives me a fright. Was it him? Me? No, the staircase's bottom flight rises. Not a soft wave like in Wellington, not a curl like at the church hall. The staircase pulls out of the floor, tiles break loose and fall around me. Up and up the staircase lifts until the entire bottom flight is in the air, railings bend and shoot up, I can't see the window any more. Then it begins to lower, now a wing. The wind pushes me off my feet, I fall backwards, I don't touch the ground, I spin round and round, wheeling like a pamphlet in a storm. I hit the wall behind me, right next to the vice-principal's office door. The wing hits the ground, the building shudders, the growl is now a raw gash in the earth. I hear his name, it's the same as mine. The mighty angel who has already seen everything is here as well. And has *my* name. Three girls walk through the lobby, they don't see the damage, they don't hear anything, two laugh too loudly and one gestures at them to be quiet.

I look at the window. The giant stands motionless. I know he saw it. His face doesn't show it, he stands there, obstinate and dangerous. I sit upright. When I stand, it will be in this world, but with newfound knowledge. The Prince is here – master and soldier – never to set foot outside his role as teacher, just to make sure that I do what I must. My protector is here, silent in a staircase, ready to split the earth every time I stumble on my way to my eventual stance in the rift between unquestionable adoration and violent rejection.

For now I remain sitting. My legs stretched out, my jacket open, my chin raised. The giant is still standing, one of those who promise happiness, or wickedness, the seducers. So many times I would succumb to ones like him, but not today.

I'm giving you a moment, I say wordlessly, That's all you can do, look at me.

Nataniël

Over the past 32 years, South African singer/songwriter/
entertainer Nataniël has written and staged 87 original
productions, released 17 albums, and published 9 collections
of short stories, 3 volumes of his Kaalkop column, 1 journal,
1 costume book and 6 cookbooks.

www.nataniël.co.za
facebook/nataniël news page
@nataniëlnews

Iolandi Pool

Iolandi Pool is a freelance editor and translator, and has
known and worked with Nataniël for many years.

www.ingramcontent.com/pod-product-compliance
Lightning Source LLC
Chambersburg PA
CBHW020151090426
42734CB00008B/780